My 12 Hours *Aren't Up Yet*

Karen M. Rosner

First published in 2023 by Onyx Publishing, an imprint of Notebook Group Limited, 11 Arden House, Deepdale Business Park, Bakewell, Derbyshire, DE45 1GT.

www.onyxpublishing.com
ISBN: 9781913206543

A CIP catalogue record for this book is available
from the British Library.

Typeset by Onyx Publishing of Notebook Group Limited.

The information provided pertaining to the years between the author's birth and their twelfth birthday was obtained from their medical charts.

To Eric, my son, who is a very intelligent young man and my pride and joy.

And in memory of my mother, a woman who always put her children first.

AUTHOR'S NOTE

Only the people who know me well know what I have gone through in the last fifty-nine years of my life, and my friend, Lory, who I have known for over four decades, has told me more times than I can count that I should write a book about my life.

So, this is it.

You should know before we get started that I was born with a congenital heart defect. This defect concerns transpositions of the great vessels, and means, in simple terms, that I was born with the blood vessels to my heart and lungs reversed. This meant I technically wasn't supposed to live to my first birthday, yet here I am, proving the doctors wrong since day one!

I'd like to share my life with those who may have a similar defect, or who have to live with some other chronic birth defect, as someone who had to learn to do the same. We're all in this together, and throughout our lives, we have to prove two things: that we have the will to live, and that we're survivors.

1
DID SOMEONE SAY "SURGERY"?

I've undergone six open-heart surgeries, and the one I remember most is the one from when I was twelve years old.

I distinctly remember going into Boston Children's Hospital for a checkup, my doctor examining me and taking the usual test, and, after the test results came back, Dr. Dick (my cardiologist) calling me and Mom into a room. He told my mother that I needed another open-heart surgery.

This would be my fifth one.

The doctor explained to us what they were going to do and how long the surgery was going to last. The surgery was known as the Mustard procedure (because a Dr. Mustard in England developed it, apparently), and though England had been performing the surgery for ten years longer than us here in the U.S., my doctor, Dr. Bernhard, had been performing this surgery more than any other doctor on the east coast.

I understood this much; the rest I didn't really absorb. I was only twelve, and the doctor was using very big words. Plus, this was adult talk, and I was still a kid. And quite frankly, I didn't want to hear the fact that I needed to be in the hospital *again*. Perhaps my logic was that if I didn't listen, it wouldn't happen. Boy, was I wrong.

I also remember the doctor telling my mother I had less than a fifty-fifty chance of surviving the surgery, and not only that, but that if I *did* survive the surgery, I'd only had twelve hours to live because the Mustard procedure was still very new in the U.S. Looking back now, I know these words didn't fully sink in at the time: I did not quite understand how dangerous this surgery was going to be, nor did I worry about my chances of survival. I was just going through yet another operation. Nothing to see here.

So, with that, my mother and the doctor set a date for the surgery, and then Mom and I went home.

When we arrived, my father asked how my appointment had gone, and my mother broke down crying. She told my father I needed another surgery and that I only had a fifty-fifty chance of surviving.

I felt bad for Mom (and sort of guilty) in that moment because she was crying, and it was kind of my fault. If I hadn't needed this surgery, she wouldn't be crying, right? So, I told her, "If me having the surgery makes you cry, I won't have it." My father told me I didn't understand (and he was right, obviously); that I needed the surgery, and that Mom was crying because she was worried about me.

Tucked up in bed that night, I could hear my mom and dad talking in the kitchen, and so I overheard most of their conversation. I can't remember much of it now, though. All I remember is a pit in my stomach as I mulled over the doctor's words: *if she does survive, she'll only have twelve hours left to live.*

That was the last time I thought of those words, however–for a while, at least. The next day, I just went on with my life, like I usually did.

Weeks went by, and my mom was preparing for us to leave for Boston.

I went into hospital two days before the surgery to get pre-operation testing done, and my aunt Julie came to the hospital the day before I was scheduled to have my surgery to be with Mom. It was during these two days that I met a little boy named Tiny. Well, that was his nickname, anyway; I can't remember his real name.

Tiny's mom (Carol) and my mom became fast friends.

Tiny had had surgery and needed to have his stitches out and to get checked out by the doctor. (In those days, if you had open-heart surgery, you had to stay in hospital for a couple of weeks, unlike today. Now, if you have open-heart surgery, you can go home just two days later.) Faced with this reality—a physical manifestation of what I was about to endure—I was getting scared, but I didn't want to tell my mother in case she got upset with me. Watching her break down after my appointment all those weeks ago had been bad enough.

It was then that the doctor came in to explain to me and Mom what was going to happen the following morning. He said that the nurse would be putting some medicine in my IV to make me sleepy, and he also warned me that I wouldn't be able to eat or drink anything after midnight. After the medicine had been administered, they would take me to the operating room and give me more medicine, which would put me to sleep and keep me asleep until the operation was over.

I asked if Mrs. Beasley, my doll (and most cherished possession), would be getting the same medicine I would, and the doctor said yes, and that she'd also have the same surgery I was having.

After the doctor left, I started to grow anxious, and I told the nurse how I was feeling. They gave me something to calm me down. You may think I would have been a veteran at this surgery stuff by now, but you must remember that this was the first surgery I'd actually understood I was having and, critically, the first one where the doctor had actually explained everything to my mother right in front of me, since I was now "old enough" to understand and to know about what was going to happen to me.

After that, the days rolled by swiftly, and before we knew it, the day of the surgery was upon us.

Everything happened like the doctor said: the nurse put some medicine in my IV, and I started feeling funny. I remember my mother repetitively telling me to lie down. I remember trying to talk with my aunt and mom and making no sense at all. I remember the people from the operating room coming to get me, and Mom and Auntie Julie walking down with us. I remember one of the nurses from the operating room jokingly asking me to walk down while they put my records on a stretcher and "wheeled them down". I had seven volumes to my medical record at that time (hence the stretcher), and this number has increased to about twelve volumes as I write today. On this day, they ended up putting the volumes on the shelf below the stretcher's bed while they wheeled me down.

Before the nurse wheeled me into the pre-op room, I said goodbye to Mom and Aunt Julie. They gave me hugs and kisses, and, looking back now, I can see that they were both worried. *Very* worried.

Once we entered the pre-op room, the nurses put a cap on my and Mrs. Beasley's heads so our hair wouldn't get in the way, and then they inserted another IV that they funneled medicine into. "Can you count backwards from ten for me, Karen?" I heard one of them say.

I don't think I even made it to nine.

That's the last thing I remember from that day. My next memory is of waking days later.

I remember not knowing where I was and not being able to talk because I had a tube down my throat and in my nose. I also, alarmingly, had wires and tubes all around me. I was a little scared over the fact that I couldn't remember having the surgery, even though I'd apparently only just had it. I felt disorientated and overwhelmed and plain out of it.

A nurse came to me and started talking to me, yet I couldn't understand what she was saying. So, I shut my eyes again.

Now, remember, I'd had less than a fifty-fifty chance of surviving the surgery, and my doctor had told my mother that if I *did* survive it, I'd probably live for only twelve hours post-surgery. Yet it had already been days after my surgery, and here I was, still alive. I wasn't out of the woods—I was still in the CCU (Cardiac Care Unit)—but I was alive, and with odds like this, that certainly counted for something.

I was *alive.*

I remember Mom telling me years after this surgery that I was too stubborn to die, and I think she was right. I'm still here, after all!

I was hooked to the tubes and wires for weeks before I was strong enough to have them removed and to be able to return to my old room.

I vaguely remember Mom, Carol, and various members of my family coming in and talking to me while I was in the CCU. That is, I remember hearing their voices, but not much more. They seemed so far away despite the fact that they were standing right next to my bed. They were talking to me, but that faraway feeling meant I couldn't make out anything they were saying. It was like a thick blanket had been thrown onto the rest of the world, muffling and blurring everything into oblivion.

When I was finally moved to a regular room, my mother cried and walked out of my room. After a few moments, Carol came in.

"What's wrong with Mom?" I asked her.

"She just had something in her eye."

I paused. "Tell me the truth."

More silence. "Your mom is just very happy to see you doing so well because you were so sick."

After this point, I got to know Carol and Tiny better, though Tiny got better faster than I did and so went home weeks before me.

About two weeks after my surgery, I was sitting with my mom in the parents' lounge on Fagan 35 when a doctor came to get me and said, "We're going to take out your stitches now." I was caught off guard with this, and he wheeled me off before I could protest, or Mom could say it was okay.

When we got to the treatment room, another little girl was getting her stitches removed, too, so, as a distraction, the doctors started "racing" (jokingly, of course) to see who could finish first. I remember screaming and wriggling because the whole ordeal hurt so badly. They hadn't hurt that badly going *in*—though then again, I'd been asleep during that. I can still vividly remember the tender stinging sensation of the doctor pulling out the stitches one by one. I was crying like crazy, and the other girl was, too.

The good part is that my doctor and I won, I think. This is my book, anyway, so we'll go with that.

After the stitches were out, I went back to my mom with tears still running down my cheeks, telling her what happened and how much it had hurt. She said she and everyone else had been able to hear me yelling.

"There was another girl in there, too, and *she* was screaming, too," I retorted. "And I don't care if anyone could hear me, anyway. It *hurt*."

This part of my stay might have sucked, but the good news was that my doctor was ready to send me home and planned to do so in two days. I was allowing myself to get seriously excited at the thought of going home and seeing my siblings, dad, and grandmother when all promises of homecoming came to a crashing to a halt: I'd developed an illness called Sydenham chorea, a movement disorder that causes involuntary, unpredictable body movements. I suddenly wasn't able to feed myself because my hands shook too much. I was disappointed that I couldn't go home, and I was also scared of this new development. The surgery had made my heart better, but now, I had to deal with this new, mysterious illness.

During this time, I played with my feet or wrung my hands constantly.

I can still picture myself and Mom at the hospital having a sundae (hot fudge, my favorite), only for me to not be able to eat it due to my hands being so shaky. Mom spoon-fed me so I could at least still have my ice cream.

My mom was visibly worried, but she never told me. Now, as a mother myself, my heart aches for my mom in these moments; how sick with worry she must have been. I also felt bad that we couldn't go home and be with the family.

To counterbalance my tremors, the hospital started me on some new medicine, and I had to stay in the hospital until this took effect. In the end, it took a couple of different medicines before they started doing the job and I was able to go home, so I actually ended up staying in hospital for two weeks longer than I was supposed to. I continued taking this medication for about a year before my doctor was confident enough to wean me off it.

When I finally returned home from hospital (which was about two months after I'd left for the surgery), I was on several different kinds of medicine, which were all to be taken at different times. I was weak, but happy to be home. That was the first time in my life I left the hospital pink in complexion instead of blue (but more on that later). It was great to be home and to sleep in my own bed, and it was even better being with my family.

Mom kept the medicine on the shelf above the sink and made sure I took each kind at the right time. She had to oversee this schedule for the full year of the course. I also saw my surgeon six weeks after I was discharged from the hospital, and upon my entering his office, the blatant surprise on his face was almost humorous. I was smiling and looking healthy for once.

"What is your name, please?"

"My name is Karen Rosner," I responded, with an evident attitude. (I could already see what was coming.)

"That can't be! She's six feet under! I only gave her twelve hours to live after her surgery."

Clearly, he thought this was a laughing matter.

I looked him in the eye and said (again, with an attitude and smile), "My twelve hours aren't up yet."

And thank God for that.

The doctor gave me a hug and a kiss on the cheek and said, "Have a nice life!" He then announced to my mother that I didn't need to see him anymore, and to continue my follow-ups with my cardiologist.

And that was that. I had passed the surgery with flying colors, and I was no longer against a ticking time bomb.

Three months after that appointment I went back to see my cardiologist, and he took me off the rest of my medications.

My surgeon ended up writing an article about my survival in a medical magazine—an article about the odds of being in favor of having the surgery. That's not to say there weren't several children who didn't survive this surgery around the same time I had it, but what can I say? I've always had the will to live! And, sure enough, it's been forty-seven years since I told my surgeon that day, "My twelve hours aren't up yet," and I'm still going strong!

I love beating the odds of things I can't control. I had zero control over the doctors' and nurses' performance during and after my surgery. Then again, my mother always got the best doctors for me while I was growing up (which very well may have come into it), though I do believe there must be a grander reason for me to still be here after a procedure like that. Don't get me wrong, my life didn't get easier after that surgery; it just became a lot easier to live life, if that makes sense. Mere months before, I'd been a sick little girl preparing for the surgery that may very well kill her, and now, I was a healthy pink little girl ready to live life like it should be: with no restrictions.

As for Carol and Tiny, Mom and I stayed connected with them for a couple of years before we lost touch. I still wonder how Tiny is doing and how his life is going; whether the surgery cured him or whether he still faces difficulties.

Tiny, if you're reading this, I hope you're living a healthy and good life.

2
FINALLY, A GIRL!

But let's backtrack to how all of this started.

Thanks to me, my mom was finally able to hear the words, "It's a girl!" on September 10, 1963.

I was the seventh of eight children to my parents, and the first girl. Apparently, my mother had previously told my father, "I'm not going to quit until I have a girl"—and she made good on her word! She then also had my sister two years after I was born, so I guess she was right to keep trying.

In my adulthood, I learned that when my mother went into the hospital to have my sister, she took me with her because she didn't want anyone else to take care of me. Which should tell you a lot about how precarious my health was from the get-go.

There were no special events that occurred during my mother's pregnancy with me. She had a C-section delivery (my brother before me, Bobby, was delivered via C-section, and in those days, once a woman had delivered by C-section, she had to deliver all her subsequent children the same way), and I weighed in at seven pounds and fifteen ounces and twenty-one inches. I had a full head of red hair (though now it's dirty blond), and my mother stayed in the hospital for ten days upon having me.

Of course, that wasn't the last time I wound up in hospital. In fact, it was probably around then—on that day my mother brought me home—that my luck ran out.

When I got home, I apparently didn't cry much. As a matter of fact, my mother said she had to physically wake me in order to feed or change me. Mom found this strange, and concluded that either there was a problem, or she'd simply been blessed with a very good baby. Not willing to take any chances on the former, she called the doctor, who didn't seem alarmed and told my mother to continue to watch me and call if there were any other problems.

It was when I was being baptized that my godfather, Tony, noticed my fingernails and lips were blue. Alarmed, my mother immediately took me to my hospital, to discover I was suffering from what was to be my first case of pneumonia. My pediatrician hospitalized me and ran some tests for a few days (you must remember this was in 1963, meaning technology was not as advanced back then), and then the doctors suggested to my mother that I be transported to Boston Children's Hospital for further testing.

So, with that, l had my first visit at Boston Children's Hospital at the tender age of nine weeks.

I also had my very first heart catheterization emergently, and it was then that the doctors discovered I had transposition of the great vessels (when the lung vessels and blood vessels are transposed backwards at birth) and a hole in my heart. Perhaps counterintuitively, the hole in the heart was what had been keeping me, and was continuing to keep me, alive. Even still, I was turning blue because my blood wasn't getting any oxygen from my lungs.

At this time, I went down to five pounds, and was still rapidly losing weight. It was also during this visit that the doctors told my parents that I wouldn't make it to my first birthday.

As I write this, I'm exactly one month away from turning fifty-nine.

For now, though, my prospects were definitely looking morbid, and since the doctors didn't want to waste any time, I had my first open-heart surgery the day after the cardiac catheterization (the one that revealed my transposition of the great vessels and hole in my heart). During this surgery, the doctors put a baffle (which facilitated my heart receiving oxygen) in my heart and closed the hole.

I was still blue after this surgery, and after I recovered, I was sent to a Good Samaritan home next to the hospital so I could gain enough weight for my next surgery.

It took me approximately nine months to gain nine ounces, and the prize I received for this was operation number two at the still-tender age of ten months—my second open-heart surgery at Children's. I don't know what exactly they did during this procedure. In my medical records, it says I had pulmonary artery banding to prevent pulmonary hypertension, so that's all I know.

After I was discharged from that round of hospitalization, the doctor requested I come back in one month for a checkup. Well, it turned out I didn't want to wait the full month: I was back in hospital two days after my discharge for twenty-four hours for vomiting.

I guess I didn't like the food Mom was feeding me!

What I'm getting at is, I was in the hospital more than I was at home for the first year and a half of my life, including my first birthday. Our routine went a little something like this: I'd come home for a few days before going back into hospital for weeks, and sometimes even months, at a time. While I was there, my mother visited me during the week and then went home during the weekend to be with my brothers and my dad.

I wasn't alone when Mom wasn't there, however: every time I went to the hospital, I'd bring my best friend, Mrs. Beasley. She was a doll from the sixties sitcom *Family Affair*, and when my mother took me to the toy store to pick out my third birthday present, I knew I had to have Mrs. Beasley the second I saw her with her matching blue polka dot apron and bib, yellow hair, and black granny glasses on the very top shelf. I immediately told my mother, "I want that doll up there." The person who worked at the toy store had some difficulties getting Mrs. Beasley down—he wasn't tall enough even when he was on the top rung of the ladder—but, with some grunting, he finally used a long pole to get the box down. Once she was in my arms, I pulled the string that was supposed to make her talk... to find she didn't work. I instantly felt my eyes fill with tears, so the poor guy, panicked, went back up the ladder to get another Mrs. Beasley.

That one talked, and *that* Mrs. Beasley was mine.

I was very happy, of course, and she was out of the box before we even got back to the car... and I didn't let go of her for eight years after that. I told Mrs. Beasley all my girlish secrets and had tea parties with her, and when we were in hospital, I'd take her to the playroom with me. I remember the nurses coming to my bed to see Mrs. Beasley, and they'd always pull her string and listen to her talk. I never let Mrs. Beasley out of my sight, and while I didn't mind the nurses pulling her string and playing with her in front of me, I'd *never* let them leave the room with her.

She had open-heart surgery whenever I did; she went to hospital every time I went. We did *everything* together and shared both the good times and the bad; the exciting and the scary. Being in hospital as a kid (or even as an adult) can be very frightening, but I wasn't even a little fearful when I had Mrs. Beasley with me.

When I was home, Mrs. Beasley was always on my bed, and I always slept with her at night... though I must admit that by the time I woke up most mornings, Mrs. Beasley was on the floor face-down.

Well, she was only a doll.

The first solid memory I have is from when I was around three years old, and I was standing in my crib watching my mother leave because visiting hours were over, crying and screaming for her to come back. (This was pre-Mrs. Beasley days, so at this point, these goodbyes were particularly traumatic.) When she turned around, I told her I wanted her to stay, and she told me she had to leave and to stop crying, or she "wouldn't come to see me the next day". Then, she turned and left.

I was scared to be alone in the dark hospital. There were lights on, but the hospital still felt eerily, suffocatingly dark.

I listened to the elevator doors opening... and then shutting again. And once I heard that definitive slam, I started crying even harder until a nurse came over to comfort me. I didn't understand then why my mother had to leave. I just wanted her to stay with me or let me go with her. Surely that wasn't too much to ask? I wanted to be with my mother, so why did she have to leave? Didn't she want to be with me, too?

Of course, I calmed down in the end, but I still always cried a lot whenever my mother left. I felt alone and scared, and this wasn't helped by the fact that she always left at night, when it was dark. Of course, she always came back the next day, early in the morning, but these goodbyes were still tremendously difficult.

I swore to myself back then that when I had a child, if they ever needed to stay in hospital, I'd always stay with them. For ever and ever and ever, if need be. I didn't want my child to be scared. I didn't want them to be alone.

My third surgery took place when I was four years old, the reason for this being I'd outgrown the pulmonary banding I'd had when I was barely one. And so, to facilitate them constructing my new shunt, I was in and out of Children's Hospital for quite a long period of time. My parents would come to take me home, and in less than one week, I'd be back in.

I also had pneumonia several times while I was growing up, and it was around this time, when I became cognizant of the fact that I constantly felt ill and was able to compare myself to my peers, that I began to properly realize that I couldn't play like my siblings or friends could. I'd get tired out quickly—far more quickly than they would—and I didn't understand why. I just wanted to play like my sister and friends did giddily and boisterously and tirelessly.

I made the best of a bad situation, playing when I wasn't tired and was feeling okay. And, looking back now, I can recall I *was* outside a lot, though I still didn't quite run around like my friends, or my sister did. Regardless, we made our own fun: our neighbor had nine kids and we had eight, so there were certainly enough of us to play with. I enjoyed being outside and loved that it allowed me to live a somewhat-normal life whenever I wasn't in the hospital or bedridden... temporarily, at least.

Yet I often felt left out because I couldn't do half the things my sister and our neighbors, including the twins (who were around my sister's age), could. I was able to ride a bike up and down the street, but only for a short time. I got tired out—no, exhausted; utterly sapped of energy—very quickly, and if I overdid it, I'd pay the price by being sick all night.

Basically, I constantly felt as though I was missing out on tons of fun, especially when I was in hospital, but also when I was out and technically doing the same things as my friends. I was just *different*, and I was reminded of this constantly.

I should mention here that as I was growing up, neither the doctors nor my mother ever told me what was going on with my health. Not that I would've been able to understand even if they *had* explained it all, but it *would* have paved the way for explaining why I couldn't do the things my sister could, even if they hadn't told me the full extent of my health issues.

What I'm trying to say is, it's strange to have more memories from your childhood that took place in hospital than at home with your family, especially when for most of that time, you couldn't even fully understand why you were there in the first place, and certainly not why you had to stay for so long and so often.

This being said, being in hospital as a kid had some advantages. For one, there were always different kids to play with, plus a supervising adult who'd join in.

One time, at age four, I was in hospital in an oxygen tank because I had pneumonia (again), and I made a friend. I can't remember his name, so we'll call him Tommy. Tommy came to my room early one morning and asked if I wanted to go to the playroom, to which I of course responded that I did, but that I didn't know how to put the rails on my crib down. So, ever the problem solver, he put a chair next to my crib and pulled the rails down for me. Delighted, I climbed down to the chair and then to the floor, and then we "ran away" to the playroom with Mrs. Beasley and played until the nurses found us. When one of them asked how we'd gotten out of bed, I told her the truth: Tommy had put the chair next to my bed and I'd climbed down.

Tommy was aghast. "She said that she wanted to come!" he protested. (Clearly, we didn't yet understand the concept of not throwing your friend under the bus!) The nurse then, of course, put us both back to bed and me back into the oxygen tent.

Well, it was fun while it lasted. At least I still had Mrs. Beasley to play with in bed!

While this may sound quite mischievous, a young child like that will do anything to play, so I'd always try to get out of bed to go to the playroom, so I didn't have to stay in bed, where it was boring. Regular hospital stays and constant illness isn't enough to suck the childhood joy from a kid, and so in all the ways that counted, I was just like any other kid... and so, naturally, I regularly got into mischief and trouble.

One example of this that comes to mind is one from when I was very small. My sister and I always played together when Mom was watching her stories, and one day, when my sister was three and I was five, we were sneakily playing in the pantry (we were supposed be taking our naps) in the cabinet under the counter, where all our canned goods were stored. The cabinet was about three feet high, two feet deep, and two feet wide, and we took most of the cans out of the cupboard—enough to fit my sister in it.

You can probably see where this one is going.

When my sister finally managed to stow herself in there, she said, "Go get Mom!" We were so proud over the fact that we had not only neatly arranged the cans on the floor, but that my sister could fit in the cabinet sitting down. We were even able to close the door with her still in it!

We closed the door before Mom came to look, and, of course, when she came to the pantry and saw all the cans all over the floor and my little sister crammed inside, she wasn't exactly amused. Actually, she got very upset with both of us. She asked me if I'd seen my sister doing this, to which I proudly responded, "I helped her."

Apparently, this was the wrong thing to say.

Just writing about this, I can still see my sister's little body curled in that cabinet, cans all around her, buzzing with pride over what we'd done. Oh, to be five again.

Another core memory from my childhood: how encouraging the hospital was of our having goals for the future. When I was about six or seven, I was at an appointment with my cardiologist, Dr. Dick, when he asked what I wanted to be when I grew up. I said, "I want to be a heart doctor!" beaming with pride.

"A cardiologist?"

"No, a *heart doctor.*"

Dr. Dick and my mother then tried to explain to me that a cardiologist was the same thing as a heart doctor... and once this message finally got through, Dr. Dick said, "Okay, write it in your chart," and gave me his pen. So, I wrote, *I want to be a heart doctor,* pausing twice to ask Dr. Dick and my mother how to spell "heart" and "doctor". When I had finished, Dr. Dick said, "Okay, now, that's going to be in your chart forever." He then explained that only important things went in my chart, and I could feel the blood rush to my face in excitement: if I could write it in my chart, it *must* be important that I become one.

Years later, I was told I couldn't be a heart doctor—a cardiologist, that is—due to my health issues. My doctors explained that healthy students have a difficult time going through med school, internships, and residency due to the stress of having to stay up for twenty-four, thirty-six, or even forty-eight hours at a time—stress that I wouldn't be able to tolerate due to my heart condition.

But at least I got to write it in my chart.

The fact that those words, written by six- or seven-year-old Karen, are imprinted in ink, is weirdly comforting to me, even if I ultimately wasn't able to pursue that career. The other thing that comforts me is the fact that I am working in the medical field and helping others, even if it isn't as a cardiologist.

So, that was my life: hospital stays and fleeting visits home. My parents always had to bring me back to the hospital only a few days after I'd returned from my last stay due to the unpredictable nature of my condition, and so it is no exaggeration to say that the doctors, nurses, housekeepers, volunteers, and clerks at Boston Children's Hospital were my second family. I celebrated many birthdays, Christmases, and Easters in that hospital, and I have a lot of memories there of the people I met and the things I did during my extensive stays.

While I (clearly) had a bit of a mischievous streak at home and in the hospital, I didn't get in trouble at school. School was for schoolwork, and *not* fooling around. That was how I saw it, anyway! Plus, I really liked school.

A school year in the Rosner household hadn't officially begun until the twins' mother (our neighbor) had taken a photo of Barbara, Mary, me, and my sister in our new outfits, ready to walk to school. After that, we'd all walk to school together—well, until high school, when I'd give them a ride instead of taking the bus.

I can remember that my first-grade teacher was tall—but then again, when you're six years old, I suppose everyone seems tall! She had blond hair that was always styled in a spiral updo, and she could *really* yell if she got mad enough. (Us kids weren't big fans of this.) She also had a soft side, though: if you were good for the day, you'd get a lollipop before going home.

Due to my condition, my first year of first grade was like kindergarten for me in the sense that I'd start school at the same time everyone else did but would go home at lunchtime, since school tired me out so much.

But I get ahead of myself.

On my first day, I walked to school (which was about six houses away from my house) with my mom and my brothers. (My sister and the twins were two years younger than me, and so were due to start two years later.) My brothers argued over who was going to take me into school (a role one of them was to be charged with, since I couldn't stand outside in the cold or go up the stairs as quickly as the other kids), and this day, my mother interrupted and said, "I'll take Karen in school. You boys wait in line until it's time to go in."

With that, Mom took me into school and spoke with my teacher and the principal, and once she left, I cried... and I continued to do this every day for the first week of school. My tears would remain a steady stream for most of the morning. My teacher, probably pretty flustered, would tell me to stop, and would then try to distract me with something else, but it just wasn't that easy. Sure, after a *while*, I'd stop, but by that point, it was time for me to go home.

After that first week, my brothers walked me to school (no Mom), taking turns to bring me in early, as per Mom's instructions, and after I got home for lunch, I would eat, take a nap from twelve-thirty until four, have supper with the family, watch a little TV, and then go to bed at around eight, from which point I would sleep all night.

Clearly, going to school took a huge physical toll on me, even if I only went for a few hours a day.

Even still, these limited hours were precious to me because it was during this time that I met my first best friend, Teresa. Teresa would call me after school to let me know what work I'd missed and whether we were going to have a spelling bee in the morning. We became such close friends that we were held back together; Teresa was out of school a lot because of her eyes. (She wore thick glasses and had to have surgery on them.)

Of course, throughout first grade (both years), I was still in and out of hospital–accompanied by Mrs. Beasley, naturally. Mrs. Beasley always came with me to the playroom, though she wasn't my only childhood love: as I grew up in the hospital, I also grew to love *Lassie.*

Another bonus of hospital life was that every Thursday night in the hospital was "movie night" for the fifth floor (also known as Fagan 35), when Bob (the "movie man") would come to the floor at about five o'clock to check out who was going to be at the movies. Bob and I quickly became pretty good friends: he'd help me to the movies if my mother wasn't there, and I remember always being excited and happy to see Bob come around asking if I was coming to the movie.

The movies were always both a happy and sad time for me because when the movie started, I knew it was my mother's time to leave for the day. Because of this, I gained somewhat of a reputation for always crying through the first few minutes of the movie in my wheelchair or go cart (long wheelchairs that us kids could lie down in) before finally settling down (probably much to everyone else's relief). We had popcorn while watching our movies (salt-free, of course, for the heart patients), and to this day, I still have a weakness for *Lassie* movies. It's strange what we hold onto from our childhoods. I actually have an autographed photo of Timmy and Lassie; a friend of mine made friends with Timmy on Facebook and told him about my story, and *voilà*, the photo became mine. *When I grow up*, I'd think in that hospital room as the movie played, *I'm going to have a dog that looks and acts just like Lassie.*

There was also Peter the "magician" that came around the hospital to do tricks for us kids. Peter was younger than Bob and newer to the hospital, and while I do somewhat remember Peter, Bob is the chief figure in my memory. After all, Bob was there practically the whole time I was.

In a nutshell, Boston Children's Hospital was great for us kids. The nurses were fantastic to me, and as I got older and came to understand my condition better, they'd explain things to me when I didn't understand the doctors and the lingo they used. They knew how to take twenty-letter words that were confusing, hard to pronounce, and foreboding-sounding, and transform them into words that felt familiar and easy to understand. The nurses also took the time with me when my mother left in the evenings to properly comfort me and calm me down. When I grew older, however, they became more like friends, and I was able to joke with them like they were friends.

Basically, I wouldn't be writing this book if it weren't for the doctors and nurses at Boston Children's Hospital, my home away from home during my childhood. Plus, being raised in a hospital had the bonus of teaching me how to get along with people of all personalities and backgrounds. After all, kids from all over the world would come to Boston Children's Hospital to have their physical problems corrected and their lives bettered. And I hope that all the children that were at Boston Children's Hospital in the sixties and seventies are happy, healthy, and living life to the fullest today.

Hospitals normally aren't the scene of happy memories for people, but I have an abundance thereof, and all because of the nurses and doctors who took care of me. And it is for this reason that I am eternally grateful to them.

3
BACK WHEN I WAS IN SCHOOL

The second year of first grade for me was a little better than the previous year, but I did still miss a lot of school. But I had the same teacher again and I was with Teresa, so we had a lot of fun: we had recess together (I'd never gone to recess the year before because I couldn't run around without a whole lot of risks to my health), and Bobby, my brother, was still in that school with me, so I got to see him during recess, too. That said, back then, the teachers wouldn't let the girls and boys play together: the boys had their side, and the girls had their side, and every week, the teacher had us switch (one side had the swings and slide while the other side had the basketball court). Despite this rule, I remember Bobby and I sitting on the school steps, talking on our own sides and chattering away.

We got in trouble a couple of times for this.

Sadly, there were many times where I couldn't go out to recess or lunch with the class, and instead had lunch in the classroom by myself. After I'd had lunch, I'd do the work that I'd missed. Not the best way to spend a recess as a seven-year-old.

Unsurprisingly, I didn't like being in the classroom alone, and I'd often have "accidents" during those times because I wasn't able to leave the room without the teacher's permission. Plus, the bathrooms were in the basement, and that was two flights of stairs away. This posed quite a big problem for me, since I couldn't go down the stairs by myself: stairs tired me out more than any other day-to-day thing, and going up *two or three flights* was like climbing the stairs to the torch of the Statue of Liberty. (Fun fact: I actually did climb the stairs to the torch a few decades later! Proof you can do anything you set your mind to.) So, I was able to go up the stairs approximately three times a day (in the morning, before lunch, and at the end of the day) at the most, but my teacher would try to limit me to twice a day. She was trying to protect me, of course, though my reaching this daily "limit", if you will, also meant I had to walk home slowly because of the slight hill at the front of our house. Not to mention the fact that it meant I couldn't relieve myself as often as I might have wanted to!

Despite missing a whole lot of school during this year, between my mother, Teresa, and my teacher, I was able to keep up with the schoolwork. It helped that I learned things that I liked quickly. I also learned a lot more in the second year of first grade than I did in the first year, and so at the school year's end, I was able to go on to the second grade. Woohoo! And the good news was that Teresa was once again in my class, *and* my sister started first grade the year I went into second grade.

Second grade was great, and I liked my teacher a lot. I distinctly remember that we learned how to add, subtract, and write in cursive. I was still missing a lot of school, but I kept up with the work relatively easily. Our system was, Mom would collect the work I'd missed, or my sister would take it home with her for me to complete at home, and I'd catch up whenever I could.

Another bonus of second grade was that my sister's classroom was right across the hall, so it was easy for her to see me. Plus, we had recess and lunch together, and now, I was able to actually go out for recess and down to lunch, which was so nice, as it meant I got to eat lunch *with other kids*! What a concept!

To make things even better, in the second grade, the boys and girls were actually allowed to play together, which proved much more fun than constantly being separated. I'd play kick soccer during recess, though I often paid for this by being sick that night or needing to go to bed at 6PM. I was just trying to be like every other kid at school, but apparently, this was too big of an ask for this body of mine. I didn't let this completely hold me back, though.

As I've mentioned, my sister and our twin neighbors (Barbara and Mary) were my main playmates when I was younger, though they all knew how to ride a bike well before I did; I was still riding my bike with training wheels by the time Barbara and Mary were riding longer and faster than I could ever imagine going.

Then, one weekend in the summer, I learned how to ride a two-wheel bike.

I was about nine years old, and was taught by the twins' older brother, Billy. I remember we started on the Saturday morning, and by the Sunday afternoon, I was riding the bike on my own. I was still yet to master the brakes–I stopped by dragging my feet–but when I was riding my bike myself, I felt on top of the world. And, most importantly, this meant I could keep up with my sister and the others riding up and down the street and going to the curve!

When I was a kid, that curve was *everything*. When I visited my childhood home before my parents sold it a few years ago, I stood outside and looked up the street and to the curve in the sidewalk, and I swear I could almost hear and see me, my sister, and the twins racing our bikes up to it and back down to the twins' house. We were laughing and I was out of breath but still having the time of my life. Life was *good*. Sure, the curve looked *much* further away when I was younger than it did now, but I suppose things do have a habit of appearing smaller as you get older. Regardless, I thought growing up on that street and riding my bike to the curve was single-handedly the best thing ever.

When we got older and had more control over our bikes, we were allowed to go to the next street over, which was great and very freeing because Mom couldn't see what we were doing! Probably a good thing, given the fact that I was partial to zooming down a very steep hill, climbing trees, and riding with no hands, which were all sure ways to give her a heart attack.

I never would've wanted to unnecessarily worry my mom, but I savored having that little bit of freedom, and so *had* to take advantage of it whenever opportunity struck.

It was also around this time, when I was about nine years old, that I got my first boyfriend... or something along those lines. I was staying at a summer camp sponsored by Boston Children's Hospital for two weeks, a camp that had been specifically set up for the kids from Children's Hospital who couldn't really participate in a regular summer camp due to their health restrictions. One quite comical (though, I suppose, expected) memory I have from this camp is the winding line of kids that was constantly outside the nurse's office every morning, noon, and night—kids collecting their medications.

If anyone had been unsure of whether or not this was a camp for sick kids before, they certainly knew it was then!

I met several new people and made lots of new friends during camp, including two boys: Albert, who had red hair and was short, a little overweight, and very nice, and Tony, who was tall and slender, with dark hair and a cute, cheeky grin. Tony, Albert and I swiftly became good friends, and I remember my new girlfriends teasing me about the fact that Tony (allegedly) "liked" me, to which I always responded, "We're just friends. I spend time with Tony *and* Albert."

Shortly after that, Albert found another group to hang around with (maybe the "third wheel" implications started getting to him!), so Tony and I started hanging out together alone.

The boys and girls had separate dining rooms, and on Tony's birthday, his mother dropped a birthday cake off at the office. At dinner that night, the girls at my table said that Tony would definitely bring me a piece of cake. I shut this down vehemently, insisting our friendship was strictly platonic.

It was after we'd said our end-of-meal prayer and right before everyone was dismissed that I got a tap on the shoulder. I turned around, and, sure enough, there was Tony with a piece of cake in his hand. He handed it to me wordlessly and walked out.

I was stunned, and felt more than a little awkward—as, it seemed, did he. My cheeks burning, I sat back down to eat the cake, and as the girls filed out of the dining room, they said, "I *told* you he'd do that!" as they passed by me. I just flashed them a smile, my heart pounding with surprise and embarrassment.

After I'd eaten my cake, I went out, to find Tony waiting for me. I thanked him for the cake, and a few days after the end of camp, Tony and I exchanged addresses, though we lost contact soon after school started.

Oh, young love!

Tony, if you're reading this, thanks again for the cake. I've thought of you often throughout the years.

*

Within the first month of third grade, I had a fat lip. On a Saturday during that first month back at school, one of my brothers and I were running upstairs so we could play a game... only there was new carpet on the stairs that was still a little slippery, and so, naturally, I missed a stair mid-stride, fell, and bit down on my lip. I started bleeding profusely and ended up in the ER with nine stitches across my bottom lip. There were a lot of liquid meals over the next few days!

My friends at school were eager to care for me when I came to school on Monday with my injury. I think I explained what had happened about one hundred times! The downside of this attention, however, was that I wasn't able to play at recess because the teachers didn't want me to fall again, so instead, my friends and I sat on the ground and talked. Not as good as playing, but definitely still an upgrade from my previous recesses catching up on schoolwork in a classroom!

The other memorable thing that happened during third grade (on a slightly more morbid note) was the teacher dying in the middle of the year. She'd been battling cancer and had sadly passed. It was hard to get used to another teacher so suddenly, and from that point, there was a taint of sorts that hung over the classroom. I also felt for her daughter, who was my age and now motherless, and suddenly felt a wave of gratitude for my own expansive family.

My fourth-grade teacher the following year was old-fashioned and quite mean. She'd usually address the students by their surname, preceded by "Miss" or "Mr.", and if she ever stepped out of the room, she'd have one of the students be "teacher" until she returned. All in all, she was a difficult teacher to please, and, again, in fourth grade, I missed a lot of school due to my heart condition. One day, she told me in front of the whole class that I had a "learning disability" because I'd answered a question incorrectly (bear in mind the fact I'd been out of school for about a week before this happened). This was deeply embarrassing, and hurt so much that that night, I told my mother what my teacher had said—and, of course, she was infuriated. The next day, she marched to the school and confronted the teacher in front of the whole class. "I heard you told Karen that she had a learning disability?"

The teacher was denying saying any such thing when another girl in class said, "Yes, you did, Mrs. Murray. I heard you say that."

The teacher was obviously not too happy about this, and after that, my mother started yelling at her. She told her how sick I was; how hard I tried to keep up with the work; the fact she sent me to school even when I wasn't feeling well because I insisted on doing so; that she didn't want me to miss too much school.

The teacher, clearly quite frazzled and taken aback, hurriedly apologized to me and to my mother, to which my mother responded, "If it happens again, I'll be going to the principal to report you."

Predictably, the teacher was nicer to me from that day and all the way to the end of the school year. As a matter of fact, she was noticeably nicer to the whole *class.* So, basically, my classmates were pretty happy that Karen Rosner's mom had come in and yelled at the teacher.

That's not to say I wasn't immune from getting into trouble from time to time. One such occasion was, funnily enough, the time I broke my shoulder. I was twelve years old, and Barbara had an old metal swing set in her backyard. One day, Barbara and I had this brilliant idea that we'd jump off a leaf pile, grab the top bar, swing, and see who could jump the furthest.

The coolest, right?

To give a picture of the area we were playing in (it is relevant context, trust me), the leaf pile was a fenced-in area where Barbara's father would dump his leaves after raking them up. The fence, meanwhile, was like thin chicken wire. Beyond the swing set, there was a grapevine that was about four feet wide, and beyond that was a foot of grass and the clothesline, which was on cement.

Yeah, you can probably see where this one is going.

Barbara went first: she jumped off the step from the leaf pile, grabbed the top bar, and swung a couple of times before letting go and landing about a foot after where the grapevine started. I watched while munching a bag of potato chips, enraptured.

When it was my turn, I rubbed my hands on my shirt to get the grease off them.

Or so I thought.

I jumped off the leaf pile, grabbed the bar, and swung—but, of course, my hands slipped off, and before I knew it, I was flying through the air for what felt like minutes. My feet eventually landed on the cement while my body landed on the grass by the grapevine. (A miracle, I see now!) Note to self: potato chip grease and metal are not a good combination. Avoid potato chips next time you feel compelled to swing from a bar and see how far you jump.

A little shaken but still giggling, I told Barbara, "I won. Now go get my mother. I can't move my right arm."

It was amid my giggles that I suddenly realized Barbara was crying. She ran to my house to get my mother, and by the time she returned with her, I was sitting up. I repeated to Mom that my right shoulder and arm felt weird, and she helped me up and walked me home. As I was walking, I turned back to Barbara and said again, "I won! I went the furthest again!" My mother, however, was upset and worried that I may have really hurt myself, so didn't share in my victory.

We sat waiting for my grandmother to come home from work (Gram always came to our house right after work), and when she finally arrived, Mom told her what had happened, and we drove to the hospital—eventually, that is. She (Gram) got lost before we arrived due to her being distracted by her worry.

Meanwhile, I wasn't in any pain and frankly didn't understand what all the fuss was about. I just couldn't move my arm the way I wanted to. No biggie.

We found out, after being in the emergency room for several hours, that I'd dislocated and broken my right shoulder, and that it had to be set and then wrapped for six weeks. And the pain certainly started when the doctor began pulling it back into place and setting it!

"She has a good set of lungs," the doctor told my mom pointedly when he was done.

An unexpected, good thing that came from the accident was that when I got home and Mom put me and my sister to bed, she sat on the floor between our beds and talked with us. She explained that the reason she told us not to do certain things was because she didn't want us to get hurt. She apologized for yelling at us so much, but explained this was just so she could protect us from harm. I really enjoyed my mom sitting there and talking with us and explaining why she did the things that she did, though this may have been less to do with the content of our conversation and more to do with the fact we were actually *having* one. It was one of the few times that she spent any quality time with us without being rushed to do something else. (Being a mom of eight, she was always busy, as you'd expect.) Don't get me wrong, she spent time with us, but this seemed... different. More meaningful to me.

I will always remember that night. I wish there had been more like that.

Before Mom put us to bed, Rosalie (Barbara and Mary's mother) came over to see how I was doing. She felt really bad for the fact that I'd gotten hurt in their yard, and apologized to Mom for what had happened, reassuring her no one else would get hurt on the swing set. She said she'd have Bill (her husband) take it down the next day. Mom told Rosalie it was no one's fault, but, sure enough, the next morning, when we were ready to go outside to play, the swing set was gone.

Ahh, well.

The other bonus that came from this was that I got to postpone my (urgent) back surgery for six weeks. That is, *I* thought it was a bonus. I don't think the doctors quite saw it that way. But more on that later.

Out of all my school years, it was fifth grade I enjoyed the most, though this was also probably my toughest year health-wise. I didn't start school at the same time as everyone else because I was in hospital having my fifth open-heart surgery (the surgery they hadn't expected me to survive more than twelve hours after). However, I was finally able to go back to school toward the end of October, though not to the same one. Instead, I was enrolled at a new school that was all on one floor, since the doctors didn't want me going up and down stairs throughout the day. Naturally, I resented this change, since none of my friends were there. Well, Teresa was, but that didn't even help matters much, since she'd already made new friends and wasn't in any of my classes.

I hated being the "new kid" and having nobody to hang out with. I was completely miserable, and, for the first time in my life, I started dreading going to school.

I told my mom I didn't want to go back; that I was alone at lunch and always cried because I didn't know anyone. I felt lonely and so out of place. Looking back now, I do think it would have been different if I'd started at the beginning of the school year, when everyone was "new", rather than right in the middle of it. Deep down, though, I just wanted to be back with my friends and in the school, I'd been going to for the past six years. So, Mom talked to the doctors, and they conceded it would be better for me to be happy than to get worked up every day. Happily, I was able to transfer back to my old school, where I had one of the new fifth grade teachers. Her name was Miss Smith (though she married toward the end of the year, and so was then known as Mrs. Williams), and she had red hair, freckles, and blue eyes. She was about five foot six, and she was very nice and *loved* to teach. I was also back with friends and my sister.

On that first day, Mom took me to school and explained to Miss Smith that I couldn't go down the stairs for lunch (again); that I had to use the principal's bathroom. The only time I could go down the stairs was at the end of the day. Hence, after someone had brought my lunch up for me, Miss Smith and I usually spent the break together, talking and eating. During these times, I learned about her, and she learned what I'd been through and what I wanted to do after I graduated school. Once we finished eating, I'd catch up on the work I'd missed from the first day of school until then, and then I'd resume lesson time with the rest of the kids.

While I had lots of schoolwork being sent home for me to complete, there was still somehow always something to do. It seemed that no matter how much I tried, there was always a *lot* of work I'd missed and needed to complete. Plus, this system of me playing catchup for previous content *while* learning new content with the rest of the class was a little confusing at times, since I was still doing work from the month before and the lesson content was way ahead of me. During lunchtime, however, Miss Smith was willing to help me and explain anything I didn't understand, and with her help, I was eventually able to fully catch up with the rest of the class near Christmas break. This took me a while, but it was worth it because it meant I could actually understand everything being discussed in class. It also meant I finally didn't have more homework than my friends, which was a *huge* novelty for me.

Now, I didn't have homework for Christmas vacation! This almost felt too good to be true. And, what's more, after Christmas vacation of that year, I was able to go out to recess *and* go down for lunch! This was great, as admittedly, I much preferred eating lunch with the other kids, though I still considered Miss Smith a friend and role model. I always dropped in to visit her during the summer when she was doing work at the school, and whenever I walked home, I'd first stop in to see her so I could tell her what was happening in my life and see how things were with her. I told her I wanted to be a doctor, a lawyer, and a writer, to which she replied, "You'll be a very busy person!" (In the end, I wasn't able to be a doctor and I decided not to be a lawyer after all, but I am a writer—and yes, I am very busy!) Miss Smith encouraged me to keep dreaming, which is something I have carried over into adulthood. Contrary to popular belief, it is *pivotal* to keep dreaming throughout your life, even (and especially) as an adult. I am fifty-nine and I still have dreams. Some I have control of and others I don't, but that doesn't mean they're not all equally important.

My old grammar school is now housing for the elderly, and whenever I drive or walk past it, I vividly recall my years in that building and the summers in the playground, and I share these memories with my son. He seems to enjoy the stories I tell from when I was a kid, and it brings me much happiness recalling these memories and reliving those (relatively) carefree childhood days.

My reason for sharing all of these anecdotes is I want to illustrate the fact that despite my condition and regular hospitalizations, I enjoyed the vast majority of my childhood. Well, the parts where I could actually act like a normal kid and do the stuff kids my age was doing, that is! I didn't really get much of that, however, and so I often felt as though I was missing out on a lot.

Sometimes, I wish I could go back to my childhood and do the things I wasn't able to do, like play hide-and-go-seek or tag for hours, be tossed in the air and get caught (hopefully), be on a team... just have no restrictions on my physical abilities. Now *that* would be cool.

So, yes, while I have many "normal" memories from my childhood and adolescence that I treasure, my condition was always at play as I navigated my daily life, and the hospital visits were literally non-stop. But that's just the nature of having a serious condition, and I certainly wouldn't say I was robbed of my childhood because of it. Nuh-uh. Sometimes, it actually enriched it because I was learning about my heart and how it was functioning before my peers were in school. Plus, I got to meet people and children that I wouldn't have met if it weren't for my condition.

What I'm getting at is, everything happens for a reason, even if we don't know what the reason for a given thing is for a long time—or ever. And it is because of that that I wouldn't change my childhood for anything.

With that said, naturally, when you grow up the way I did, you find yourself questioning many things about your identity–like, would I be a different person if I hadn't had to live with my heart defect all my life? Would I have a different career to the one I have now? To what extent did my environment and defect influence my life choices? In truth, as I write this, I think my defect and environment both played a massive role in how I came to do what I do today... though who really knows the true extent of this influence? All I *do* know is that it's impossible to go back in time, so to compensate, I spend today living the life my younger self would have wanted for future me. I do *what* I want, *when* I want. (Well, to an extent.) Yes, I still have physical restrictions, but I'm more stubborn now, and I don't have my mother constantly around, so at times, I push myself beyond these restrictions. And yes, at times, I pay for not listening to the doctor and end up in bed with a headache or just plain exhaustion. Will I ever learn? Maybe; maybe not. But am I having fun? Hell yes. I live life to the fullest!

My doctors have learned throughout the years that it's better to *suggest* what I should and shouldn't do than to *tell* me not to do something. They have a much better success rate that way!

Bottom line: I'm trying to stay healthy *and* to live a normal life; to not make myself sicker and my life more difficult while still living life as fully as I can. I feel that is the most important thing. Because of this, I always take my medication, without fail, but I also push my body to its limits. Because what is the point of a life half-lived?

4
STAND UP STRAIGHT

It was discovered when I was eight years old that I had a very severe case of scoliosis (curvature of the spine). They couldn't do surgery to resolve it at that time because of my unstable heart, so instead, they fitted me for a brace (known as the Milwaukee brace), which I had to wear twenty-four hours a day, seven days a week. The only time I could take it off was when I went swimming or bathing.

The brace covered everywhere from my chin to my thighs, and the part that went around my thighs was made of heavy plastic. There were two steel bars in the back and one steel bar in the front, a steel ring around my neck with a plastic chinrest, a belt at the bottom of the back to attach the brace securely, and a strap in the middle that went under my arm so the brace wouldn't move from side to side. *That* was the most uncomfortable part of the brace. Then again, the screw that sat on the back of my head did have the bad habit of pulling on my hair, so it maybe would've been a strong contender.

Clearly, this was the pinnacle of fashion and coziness.

The brace was extremely uncomfortable at first, and I never really got used to it. And this wasn't helped by the fact that I'm allergic to plastic—I break out in rash whenever I touch it, never mind when I'm wearing it 24/7—so I always had sores on my hips and under my chin. Mom tried to fix the chinrest so I wouldn't break out from the plastic, and I'd often wear a long men's T-shirt to prevent the plastic from rubbing on my hips, but this did little to mediate the constant discomfort I was in.

I can definitely be forgiven for saying I didn't like wearing it one bit. It pulled my hair and irritated my skin, and worst of all, people would stare at me when I was out in public. I felt different and as though everyone was talking about me, and I didn't *want* to be different. I wanted to be like everyone else: unnoticed.

Eight to thirteen were probably the hardest years I went through entirely because of the brace. When I wore it, I walked funny and couldn't move my head, which only served to add insult to injury, and my rash breakouts were at an all-time high.

When I see someone in a similar brace now, I can sympathize, and I try not to stare at them because I know how it feels to just not want to draw attention to yourself but to be faced with no choice. Though I must admit that when I do look at them, I wonder if I really looked like that when I wore my brace, since it undeniably does look a little strange.

In a nutshell, my brace made me an easy target for people to stare at or make fun of, and I detested it accordingly.

I was happy about my having surgery—the back surgery, I mean—since this would mean I wouldn't have to wear the stupid, uncomfortable brace anymore (which should put into perspective quite how much I hated the damn thing. I was excited to have *back* surgery just so I wouldn't have to wear it for a bit!). And it seemed the doctors were just as eager as I was. After my fifth heart surgery, my orthopedic doctor started talking more and more about my impending back surgery, since my spine was only worsening. They were anxiously awaiting my cardiologist's go-ahead.

Ultimately, the doctors decided to complete the surgery in October—that is, October 1976, when I was thirteen years old. Before this, the doctor of course explained the procedure to me and my mom, a discussion I felt more confident during than that which we'd had before my heart surgery. After all, I'd known I was going to have this surgery for a while, and I knew by this point what questions to ask, so I felt way more prepared for this conversation and surgery as a whole. I asked how long I'd be in the hospital for and what was going to happen to me during it—all the standard questions—and the doctor explained that I would be in hospital for two days before the surgery so they could do some pre-op testing, go through the whole explanation again, and tour the recovery unit and the specific floor I'd be on. He also emphasized that he wanted to do the surgery as soon as he could, considering how much my back was worsening. He said if my spine curved another five degrees one way, I'd be paralyzed for the rest of my life, and if it curved five degrees the *other* way, it could be fatal. He explained that he was accordingly going to make an incision that curled a little at the end from the back of my neck to my tailbone, and that they were then going to put a metal rod the length of my spine alongside my spine and screw it in place. This rod would allow me to grow throughout the years. He also said I'd be in a body cast for six to eight months post-surgery, until my back fully healed.

No problem, I thought. *It's going to be cold outside, so I'll have an extra layer warmth for the winter.* (Remember, I lived in Massachusetts, where the winters are bitterly cold!)

So, as planned, the surgery was scheduled for late October. My mother signed the necessary paperwork, and it was a done deal—and before I knew it, it was two days before the surgery and I was being admitted to Boston Children's Hospital, this time on the sixth floor, not the fifth. I was scared over being placed on this floor, considering most of the patients were either in bed or in a cast. I distinctly remember seeing a kid in bed who was very overweight, in a body cast, and literally couldn't move and was crying out in pain, and, in that moment, I was deeply afraid over the fact that in a mere matter of hours, I'd be like him: immobile and in immense pain.

At that moment, the doctor came into my room to explain again what was going to happen during the surgery. They explained to me the type of bed I was going to be on (a Stryker stretcher) and said I could even try it out before the surgery, if I wanted. This stretcher was designed for the patient to lie on and have another cover (if you will) with holes for the face and arms placed over them, at which point the covers would be bound together with screws at the head and feet and the stretcher flipped over, so the patient was facing the floor.

Of course, I wanted to give the stretcher a try before the surgery, and, somewhat surprisingly, I found the turn to be smooth. I felt like I was on a ride at an amusement park.

On the day of the surgery, I was medicated the same way I had been when I'd had my heart surgery: first, I had something to calm me down in my room, and then I went to the operating room, where the anesthesiologist gave me something stronger to help me to sleep.

The surgery itself went fine; it was after surgery when the problems started.

I awoke a few days after the surgery, and immediately (startlingly!) saw a huge Easter Bunny and Dorothy before me. (Yes, really.) And no, I wasn't hallucinating, but I certainly thought I was! It turned out it was just Halloween and the nurses were dressed up, though suffice to say I was very confused when I came out of my drugged-up stupor in a strange room with the Easter Bunny and Dorothy casually parading around. It was only when a nurse came over to wish me a happy Halloween that I put the pieces together.

I also found I now didn't like the Stryker stretcher so much. I was in a not-insignificant amount of pain, and I didn't like the fact that I never knew who was in the room with me until they stood right next to my bed. And this was made worse by the fact I was on that stretcher for *two weeks* after the surgery so my back could heal a little before they put the cast on. The nurses had to flip me every two hours so I wouldn't get sores on my back or buttocks, and I hated when the time came for me to be back on my stomach.

When I was recovering from my surgery in the ICU, I was heavily medicated so I wouldn't feel any pain, and the medicine definitely did its job: I couldn't feel *anything*. Not even my legs, arms, or feet. I only knew I still *had* arms and legs because I could see them. Otherwise, I would've had no idea. The doctors would often come in to do a neurological test and would put a pin up the middle of my foot, and I wouldn't even feel it. (Today, if a doctor tries do that, my toes curl in before they even have the chance to touch my foot. My feet are now really hypersensitive, probably because of this experience.) The feeling to my legs and feet came back gradually, though—to my relief! As the doctor described it, they'd operated on the spine, and because all the nerves in the body are connected to the spine, all the feelings come back once the spine is fully healed.

During this period, something happened that my mother doesn't know about even to this day. At least, I don't believe so.

One night, while I was heavily medicated, I dreamt that I was at home and I was going from my bedroom to the kitchen—to find layers and layers of spiderwebs hanging over it, preventing my entry. So, I swung at the spiderwebs, trying to break them so they wouldn't get in my face. As I was doing this in my dream, I subconsciously noted that I could hear alarms and bells, and, finally, a nurse woke me up.

During my dream, I'd taken all the tubes out my mouth and nose, the IV out my arms, and every other wire that was on me off. The nurse asked what was wrong, and I told her there were spiderwebs in front of me. And then, pulling myself together a little and taking in my surroundings, it dawned on me what I'd done, and I, horrified, begged the nurse not to tell my mother, or she'd be upset. She told me that she had to tell the doctor, so I asked her to beg the *doctor* not to tell my mother instead. And, sure enough, when the doctor came in and saw what I'd done, he promised me he wouldn't tell my mother what had happened, on the condition that I let him, and the nurse put the tubes back in.

"Sure. Fine."

There was one unforeseen circumstance that occurred as a result of this, however: since I'd now had the tubes pulled out, put back in, and later (before I was discharged), pulled out again, my left vocal cord was completely ruined. Specifically, it became paralyzed. I couldn't really speak above a whisper, and, naturally, this prompted questions from my mother. The doctor told her that they may have given me too much oxygen and caused damage to my vocal cords, and that when I turned eighteen years old, they'd repair it for free. My mother accepted this explanation, and the doctor winked at me as we left the hospital.

From that point, I had a hoarse voice for decades, and people would always ask me if I had a cold. "No, this is my normal voice," I'd respond, to which a sheepish apology would always follow. I must admit that it was annoying and frustrating at times to have to explain to absolutely everyone about my voice. I finally had my voice repaired in my late forties, and now, I have an implant in my throat that moves my left vocal cord over, meaning when I talk, I still have somewhat of a raspy voice, but it (thankfully) doesn't sound like I have a cold all the time.

The other thing that proved difficult after this surgery was the fact that I didn't stop bleeding for a while. The doctors regularly gave me several units of blood to replenish what I had lost... only for them to grow concerned at the rate at which I'd lose it again. And it wasn't only my physical symptoms that was concerning: I was also quickly losing interest in everything. I didn't want to play with Mrs. Beasley or talk to anyone. My mom bought me a new doll, and I didn't even want to play with that.

My brother, Allen, came to see me during this time and told me not to give up and to get better soon.

Finally, my body started to accept the blood, and as soon as I stopped bleeding, I started to get stronger every day.

Then, they put my post-surgery cast on me. The cast weighed twenty-five to thirty pounds and was three to four inches thick.

Basically, it was a beast.

And to add to this, back in 1976, the cast was plaster and had no coating (like today's casts have), meaning it was actually heavier than my normal weight at thirteen years old.

After the cast dried (which took a few days), the hospital's physical therapist came to my room to teach me how to walk with it on. At first, I did this with crutches so I could have that extra support, and after about a week, I could walk without them. And from that point, it was time to begin my post-surgery life... again.

I remember the cast being really heavy and uncomfortable at first. Regardless, I had to get on with it. What other choice did I have?

The doctor cut out a circle of the cast where my stomach was so it could expand when I ate, and I learned to walk quickly, despite the strangeness and discomfort of my new adornment. The truth is, I was determined to learn to walk quickly because I knew once I could, I could go home. And, soon enough, I walked out of the hospital without my crutches an inch taller than when I walked in (the rod, remember!), not without difficulty, but with my head held up high.

The hospital also sent me home with a special pair of non-prescription glasses with a mirror on them. I couldn't bend my head down due to the cast, but with these glasses, I was still able see the ground and where I was walking, or my desk where I was completing schoolwork, while still looking straight ahead: I'd put the glasses on, and they would reflect anything below my neck. These glasses looked funny, but they were cool in the fact that they eliminated one of the main issues I would've faced post-surgery: losing my sight.

Plus, no one else in my class had a pair—naturally. Which felt cool.

The first couple of weeks I had the cast on for were difficult, but after that point, I got used to it. It became part of me, in a way. Plus, it had the bonus of keeping me warm during the cold days of winter, as I'd predicted. From a social perspective, however, it remained difficult to wear, considering I was treated differently for it: I had to ride a bus for the handicapped to school and back because I couldn't see the ground in the normal way (which meant my mother didn't want me to walk to school); I had to have someone walk me to my classes; I had to leave classes five minutes early so I wouldn't get caught in the crowd and get pushed or trip and fall in the hall. Plus, kids that didn't know me made fun of me and said I was a freak.

Kids can be so cruel to each other. I tried to fit in as much as possible, but I couldn't exactly do much about my social standing while I had the cast on.

Even still, my friends often volunteered to walk me to my classes and the bus before the end of the school day, and they didn't make fun of me. This didn't do much to soften my feelings toward school, though. In fact, I *hated* going at this point because I was so relentlessly teased by others. And my sister (unintentionally) made this worse for me at one point: she signed *Debra* across the top of my cast in big, black letters, and one day, I wore a thin shirt... and the *bra* at the end of *Debra* was the only part you could make out through it. The boys made fun of me from that day forward. Needless to say, I didn't wear that shirt again.

I don't wish to imply that having the cast was all doom and gloom: it kept me warm, I had a full-body shield during snowball fights, and I gained twenty-five pounds without eating a thing (something I viewed as a bonus). The bad points were that it was uncomfortable, it was *very* itchy, and I couldn't wash my hair or shower normally. Because of the latter, I had to go to the beauty salon once a week to get my hair washed, since I couldn't bend my head forward enough for my mother to wash my hair in the sink or bathtub. In between salon trips, I would make do with dry shampoo, which frankly sucked: it made my scalp unbearably itchy. My whole body was *already* itchy, and now my *head* was itchy, too? What kind of sick joke was that? Then again, I did revel in the fact that I felt like a "real" adult going to the salon to get my hair done.

This brings us to another interesting story from around this time: in the middle of winter, my friend Barbara and I were having a snowball fight. I don't know who was winning, but we were certainly having fun. Barbara threw a snowball at me, and I turned sideways and lifted my head slightly off the cast's chinrest. The snowball hit the chinrest and proceeded to partially fall down my cast—and boy, did that feel good!

"Don't tell your mother!" Barbara said quickly. "She'll get mad." (Getting the cast wet was a big no-no.)

"Could you do it again? In the back this time?"

"No!"

And just like that, the snowball fight was over.

I still don't know who won. I guess I did, since she was the one to quit. Barbara, if you're reading this, feel free to correct me!

I had to have the cast changed after three months, and this meant I had to stay in the hospital for three days. This hospital stay was easy: the first day I was there, they sawed off the cast (which, by the way, made a *lot* of noise, which was a little alarming), after which I was out of the cast for a full day, back on the bed I'd been on immediately after I'd had the surgery. This time, it wasn't so bad, but that was only because I wasn't in pain anymore. Every other aspect was just as I'd remembered it.

During this hospital stay, I at one point saw the X-ray of my back, including the rod, and thought it looked cool.

"You're the first girl that's said it looks cool! Other's just thought it was gross," the doctor laughed.

On this blessed day, my mom was also able to give me a sponge bath and lather some lotion on my back and stomach. This joy was short-lived, though: even though I now had the cast off, I wasn't supposed to move much, so I spent the second day largely trying to stay immobile. Then, on the third day, they put another cast on. This cast seemed heavier at first, but the doctors assured me it was the same size. I then had to stay in the hospital for *another* day, until the cast dried thoroughly, so they could cut out the stomach hole and make any necessary adjustments. It wasn't until the fourth day that I was finally sent home.

It took less time for me to adjust to this cast than the first one, yet about one week after I left hospital, I ended up in the emergency room in another nearby hospital. I'd noticed and told my mother that my right leg hurt and felt funny, and she'd told me to go lay down before supper; that I just needed to rest.

Mother knows best!

Mom then called me for supper, and when I got off my bed, I fell to the floor (literally). I couldn't feel my right leg and, thinking it had gone to sleep, I tried shaking it, but this didn't help. All I could feel was a whisper of pain that felt weirdly numbed and distant, so I called my mom into my room so she could help me off the floor. When she lifted me up, I tried to stand, but found, astoundingly, that I couldn't put any weight on my leg whatsoever.

My father had already arrived home for supper, so he took me and Mom to the hospital. When we got there, he grabbed a wheelchair for me, and, once I'd been wheeled in, the doctor in the emergency room took X-rays of my leg and found I had a case of bursitis. He said I was the youngest case he'd known of it. He gave me a shot of cortisone in my hip and cut the cast a little more so it wouldn't dig into my leg when I sat down.

By the time I got home, I was able to walk again—thank God for doctors!—and Mom, Dad and I finally got to have our supper. (Gram had kept it warm for us. Thank God for doctors *and* Gram!)

The winter that followed was a characteristically bitter one, yet I only ever wore a light jacket to school. Yes, it was freezing out, but I had a twenty-five-pound cast on that kept me warm, plus a hat and gloves. What I had failed to consider, however, was how this came across to other people, considering my siblings always arrived at school bundled up. It therefore shouldn't have come as a surprise when my mom soon got a call from the school wondering why I was coming to school with a light jacket on while my siblings were coming to school with padded winter jackets! Mom explained that I was warm enough with the light jacket due to the cast, and, thankfully, the teacher understood and dropped the subject. The last thing we needed was CPS being called in for suspected neglect!

Another funny incident that arose as a result of the cast went something like this: about one week before school ended, I remember my sixth-grade teacher, Mrs. Brosseau, telling a few kids to straighten up and not slouch. One of the kids then asked her, "Why don't you ever tell *Karen* to straighten up?" to which the teacher replied, "Karen is always sitting up straight." And that was true—obviously! I always sit up straight now; I can't even slouch if I want to. It's just instinctive after so much time spent in a cast!

There are also some other amusing stories from the period immediately after I got my cast off. I was (again) sitting in my seat in Mrs. Brosseau's class one day when a couple of the guys started throwing around their sneakers wrapped up in a gym towel. When one kid launched the towel, it hit my right side–which hurt because he'd thrown it hard. I started crying and went to the nurse, and the two kids that had been throwing the towel around went to the principal's office.

Thankfully, I was okay; no damage was done. No further cast needed for me!

Another time, I was in the playground playing with a friend of mine when another girl arrived, came up to me, and slapped me as hard she could in the back.

I swung around and punched her in the jaw. I meant to hit her on the arm.

A couple of my brothers saw the whole thing. Meanwhile, me and the other girl were crying, because my back really hurt, and she... well, she'd just been punched.

I was kicked out of the playground by the counselor there for a couple of weeks, and when my brothers and I arrived home with me crying still, we explained everything to my mother, who was furious at the counselor. So furious, in fact, that she went to the counselor's home, gave her a piece of her mind, and said that she'd be going to the parks and recreation office in the morning to explain what had happened (i.e., that the counselor had kicked me out of the playground and not the other girl who started it).

In the end, Mom stuck to her word, and headed over the very next morning to put a complaint in against the counselor. Sure enough, they kicked the other girl out of playground for two weeks, too, and the counselor was henceforth under supervision with a senior counselor at the park.

The girl and I apologized to each other in the end, and the happy ending is we never hit each other again. (Hurrah!) We were not good friends, but we were certainly friendly to each other from then on, and actually ended up graduating high school together.

The best part? My niece and the girl's niece are best friends today. Plot twist of the century!

This is the last notable cast-related event I can recall before it finally got it taken off in late May/early June of that year. I can remember that it was warm out and we had our pool open, and I was dying to jump into it now my cast was off. First, though, I had to relearn how to walk without the extra twenty-five pounds, and I also had to re-remember that I could now move my neck up and down—a little disorientating after so many months of not being able to! Swimming could definitely wait.

I got the cast off just before the end of school, just as the weather getting warmer. What timing! I had to stay in the hospital for two nights to get it taken off, but no matter: when I returned, I went straight to Gram's house and took a very long, warm, enjoyable shower. Gram knocked on the bathroom door a couple of times to make sure I was okay, I was in there for so long! Remember, I hadn't taken a shower in about seven months, so it felt *beyond* luxurious. When I stepped out, I felt like a new person.

Though I was fine from this point, I still continued taking the bus back and forth to school (it was the end of the school year), since now, without my cast, I looked at what I'd previously perceived as the annoyances of my condition in a different light: it was a way to get out of school fifteen minutes earlier than anyone else!

Six months after the cast was removed, I saw my surgeon again, who told me I was doing excellently and that I didn't need to see him again unless I ran into trouble. The rod wouldn't need to be removed unless there was a problem, and besides, they figured I'd been through enough surgeries in my short life, so why have me go through another one?

I don't know about the doctors, but as a patient, surgery is not so fun, so this was the best news ever. I was finally out from under doctors' care for the first time my life, meaning I could finally be a kid with no restrictions for the very first time in my life!

I felt truly free, and it was incredible.

5
TO BE YOUNG AGAIN

The seventh grade was when I started having heart problems again.

I first noticed that something was amiss when I was sitting in my English class one day. I suddenly felt my heart start racing–and not because the teacher was good-looking! A little alarmed, I raised my hand and asked to go to the nurse's office, and upon receiving my teacher's go-ahead, I stood up... and instantly felt dizzy. I then asked the teacher if someone could walk me there, and everyone in the class raised their hand to volunteer. I wish I could say this was because of my unrivalled popularity, but the truth is this teacher wasn't exactly exciting or good at keeping a class engaged, so everyone was dying to have an excuse to leave.

When I got to the nurse, she took my pulse, to find its BPM was at one hundred and thirty. She called my mom, who picked me up and took me straight to the local hospital. Once there, it was quickly established that my heart was out of rhythm and going too fast, so I stayed the night. My dad took me and Mom to Boston Children's Hospital the following morning, where I stayed for ten days. (Mom and I usually traveled to Boston by bus, but Mom wanted Dad to take us this time just in case I got worse, and we had to stop at another hospital along the way.)

I was quite a trouper when it came to health scares at this point, but I must admit it *really* didn't feel good when my heart was racing like it was. I felt short of breath, weak, and really, really out of it.

During that stay, the doctors tried to find a medication that would control my irregular and fast heartbeat. I wasn't on any medication at this time—I hadn't been for a little over a year—but I'd been having annual checkups with my cardiologist. When they finally found an effective medication, I went home, and this was a very welcome return home indeed: when I arrived, I found a new bike waiting for me. My sister had gotten one, too, and, to my joy, I got to ride the bike no problem since I was on my medication again, though the problem with my heartbeat persisted. The doctors called it atrial flutter, meaning the atrium was pumping faster than it should be. So, basically, I went from being on no medication for over a year to being on about three again within a matter of hours. I wouldn't have minded this sudden change if it weren't for the side effects I always had to deal with when adjusting to a new medication. This process could be draining, and the symptoms were never fun.

In the end, I wound up in hospital quite a few times for this problem (my atrial flutter) and, as a result, I missed a lot of school, as per usual.

It was also in the seventh grade that I met Robin. Now entering adolescence, I was becoming a little more rebellious, and Robin was my one friend throughout junior high and some of high school. Robin and I did everything together: wherever Robin was, I was right behind her. Yet my mother never liked Robin or approved of our friendship. She thought Robin was bad news, and, due to her trepidation surrounding the entire friendship, she never liked me going to her place overnight. She'd only let me go if I asked her more than once, or if there was something going on at my house. But this didn't stop me and Robin from becoming friends fast: we shared the same interests and got on like a house on fire almost immediately. Robin and I were kind of like opposites, and you know what they say about opposites! Robin cursed all the time, whereas I never did—well, before I met her, that is. I liked school, and she hated it with a passion. She was intelligent and a very fast reader but didn't like sitting in the classroom and ended up quitting school at sixteen, while I'd always loved school and was relatively studious. And yet we had a real bond. Plus, she was the one who introduced me to Rod Stewart, who I still listen to today and who I have seen live eight times, so she definitely gets some best friend points for that!

Saying this, Mom might not have been entirely inaccurate with her gut feeling: Robin and I got into situations that we shouldn't have but didn't know better to avoid. One time, we hitchhiked in our town because it was raining, and some guy picked us up. I sat in the front with this guy while Robin nervously blabbered about how her mom would be waiting for us when we got there. When the guy (mercifully) dropped us off close to her house, we laughed and agreed that it had been a stupid move.

Basically, I started to spread my wings a little during this time, or, at least, I tried to. And it was also around this time that Jim and I got closer.

When I was about eleven or twelve, I'd been hospitalized due to my irregular heartbeat, and now, at fifteen, Jim (a fellow patient) and I talked all the time whenever we were in the hospital together, comparing stories of what we'd been through.

One night, Jim ordered a "meat-lover" pizza for us—something that wasn't permitted on either of our diets because of the salt—and when the nurses found out, they weren't too happy. Jim, smooth as ever, just said, "Don't worry, we got a large, so we'll share it with you guys." And, sure enough, the nurses let us have one slice each before they took the rest—though when the nurse wasn't looking, Jim took two more slices and hid them until the nurse left the room. We laughed hysterically as we ate our forbidden second slice of pizza.

We also had fun talking and learning about each other's health problems, and after we were discharged, we wrote to one another.

At one point, I ended up in hospital again when Jim happened to be at another hospital down the street at the same time, so we talked to each other on the phone pretty much constantly. One night, during one of these calls, Jim asked if I was hungry, and I said yes, so he ordered me a small pepperoni pizza, an ode to our previous act of mischief. When the nurse saw it come to my room, she asked me if I'd ordered it. I (truthfully, mind) told her no, so she asked where it had come from, and I nonchalantly gave her the name on the box (mine).

"Who ordered it, then?"

"I don't know."

Another nurse then came into my room with the discovery that Jim was at the hospital down the street. Onto our scent, the nurse asked if Jim had ordered the pizza.

"I don't know." (I understood the concept of throwing your friends under the bus by this point, and I wasn't going to do that to Jim.)

Again, they let me have a slice, I secretly took another slice, and they had the rest.

Years later, I went back to Boston Children's Hospital as a patient, to find it had changed so much. (They still took me on despite my being an adult because I started my care there when I was a baby, and I still had a congenital heart defect.) It was a totally different building, and it wasn't called Fagan 35. A couple of the old familiar nurses were still there, however, and during my hospitalization, one of my old nurses asked if I had any money with me.

"No," I answered. (I kept my purse at home.) "Why?"

"Because I don't want you ordering pizza again."

We both laughed. "I can honestly say I never ordered the pizza."

"I know, because your mother never left you with any money. Jim ordered it." She smiled sadly.

"Do you have proof?" (Again, not throwing my friend under the bus. See, I'm learning!)

"No."

We laughed again.

After Jim and I were discharged, we started writing to each other again, and in these letters, Jim would often send me his drawings. He was good. Like, really good.

Then, for a while, I didn't get any letters from him.

It was about a year after that last discharge and a couple of days after Valentine's Day when Jim's mother called my mother to let her know that I wouldn't be getting any more letters from Jim because he'd passed away on Valentine's Day. She said he'd died in his sleep. My mom told me that Jim's mom had said that he'd always talked about me and was happy every time a letter from me arrived.

I now know that it was better for Jim for his suffering to end, but when I found out, I didn't know how to feel. I cried a little bit, and then went on—not because I wasn't deeply rattled, but because I had to. I was upset, both at the situation and at myself because I'd carelessly thrown out the old drawings and letters Jim had sent to me just a few days before I got this news.

I do remember feeling sad the next time I ended up in hospital because I knew Jim wouldn't be there, yet there was also fear mixed up in my feelings—fear that it could happen to me at any time, too. Jim's death really brought that ever-present possibility home for me.

Regardless, I'm thankful that I met and got to know Jim. He was a talented artist and aspired to go to art school.

I met other kids during the years I was at Boston Children's Hospital, of course, but they didn't make as much of an impact on me as Jim did.

The day after my sixteenth birthday (I didn't want to work on my birthday!), I got my first job at the local nursing home.

I remember my very first day on the job very distinctly. I was walking down the hall with a classmate (who had started the same day) when we saw a woman with blue hair sitting in a wheelchair smoking a cigarette.

"Does that woman have blue hair?" I whispered excitedly.

She replied, in a surprised voice, "Yes!"

And that was my introduction to working with the elderly. *This is going to be interesting,* I thought, bemused.

Well, I was certainly right about that!

I was assigned to the C wing in the nursing home, and after report, I was paired up with a girl name Lory. She'd been working there for about a year and had been chosen to show me the ropes. And, as luck would have it, we became fast friends, and we're still friends to this day. (She's the Lory I mentioned in the Introduction!)

Lory showed me how to pass out the linens to each resident before getting them ready for dinner, among the many other things you needed to know for the job, for two weeks. Then, my orientation was over, and I was given my own assignment.

Only two months after I started, I had a resident die in front of me. She hadn't been doing well, but often bounced back, suddenly becoming very talkative or wanting to get out of bed.

On this particular day, I had no concerns before going into the resident's room so I could change her.

And then I noticed she wasn't breathing or responding.

I called for the others to come in the room, crying and gripping the bed rails very tightly in my panic.

When the nurse in charge of the unit arrived, she hurriedly told someone to get me out of the room, and, before I knew what was happening, one of the aides was prying my hands off the bedrails, taking me down to the sitting room, and helping me calm down. Once I started to gain composure, I asked her what the next step was, and she told me that the aide would have to clean the resident up, tag her, and help put her in a body bag.

"I want to do that," I said firmly. "Will you do it with me?"

She nodded.

With that, she and I went back to the room, where two other aides had already begun the process under the supervision of the charge nurse.

"I want to do this," I told the charge nurse.

"I'm afraid not."

"I'll clean the resident up or do whatever else needs to be done."

"I'm sorry, but not this time."

"She needs to do it," the aide I'd just spoken with interjected, "and I'll be helping her."

The charge nurse finally relented, and while I couldn't help but cry while I cleaned the resident, I knew I had to do this. It also had the surprising benefit of helping me process the situation a little better, and I was comforted by the knowledge that the resident was being treated gently throughout the process.

I learned very quickly that this part of my job was my least favorite. But that isn't to say the job didn't have its fun moments.

In the eighties, you were allowed to restrain a patient if you thought they might harm themselves or others (questionable by today's standards, I know), and the restraints were said to work seamlessly. And I can personally attest to this. There was a day just before dinner when we found a Geri chair with a posey restraint sitting near the nurse's desk, and I plopped onto it, curious to test it out, when Lory and another aide suddenly started tying the posey restraint behind the chair, putting a vest restraint on me, and sliding the table attached to the Geri chair in front of me so that I was well and truly wedged in.

I was totally locked into the chair, and, giggling like maniacs, they ran away.

A few moments later, the night supervisor came along and found me in my very degrading position, restrained in the Geri chair, and asked me what I was doing. I very quickly (while trying not to giggle at the ridiculous situation I'd been found in) said, "I'm testing the restraints, and they all work just fine."

It was an interesting feeling being restrained with no one around to help! Maybe "helpless" would be a better word. And while this had, of course, just been a lighthearted prank, it meant I was then able to understand how the residents of the nursing home must have felt when we used these restraints on them.

"Glad to hear it," the night supervisor said with a frown. "Now get out of that and bring the residents to dinner."

Okay, sure thing.

Lory and the other aide excitedly asked what the supervisor had said, so I relayed the conversation onto them. Hysterically laughing, Lory and the other aide let me out of the restraints, and we were still giggling when we brought the other residents down to dinner.

This wasn't the end of our pranks on one another: Lory, myself, and the other aides would all play pranks on each other all the time, especially on April 1. Funnily enough, this did wonders for the residents, who laughed whenever we joked around with each other. Sometimes, we'd even get the residents involved in our pranks.

One April 1, when Lory and I were working, I went into one of Lory's residents' rooms and filled the bedpan up with water a couple times–to Lory's utter confusion. Later, Lory came to me and said, "That resident has filled the bedpan up *again*!" I spilled the beans in earshot of another resident, who laughed heartily.

She got me back, though, and good! Soon after this, she went into one of my residents' rooms and hid her handgrips. I knew this resident's routine very well: she needed her pillow a certain way, and after she was changed, she wanted a little perfume on her, her covers to be pulled up just below her chin, and her handgrips placed in her hands. So, later, when I came to complete this ritual, I was bewildered when I couldn't find her handgrips. I looked all over her and her sister's living area (they shared a room) and simply couldn't find them. She kept asking for them, and I told her I'd ask if anyone else had seen them... to no avail. No one had any idea where they were.

Well, *almost* no one.

In that moment, I knew Lory must have had something to do with it.

The penny dropped right at the end of my shift, and—surprise, surprise—when I asked her, Lory followed me into the resident's room with me and took the handgrips off the top shelf of the closet, where I couldn't see or reach.

The resident was happy to have her handgrips back, and Lory and I laughed hysterically. She'd made me go on a wild sheep chase alright. That was the day that I learned you had to be able to take what you dished out!

Another funny memory involving Lory went like this: Lory and I would often give each other rides to work if we were having car trouble, and there was one such time when she came to pick me up in her brother's Mustang. It was raining, and the windshield wiper on the driver's side wasn't working, so Lory had to drive *while leaning toward the passenger side* so she could see out the window while I navigated.

Then, it started to rain harder.

She drove slowly while I continued to navigate, and, by the grace of God, we somehow got to work safely. We were in our late teens, and we clearly thought we were invincible, laughing as we crawled through the blistery streets, unable to see even a few feet in front of us.

Lory and I still chuckle when we talk about this. The story conjures a very comical image, even if it could have ended very badly!

It's funny now comparing my friendship with Lory to my friendship with Robin and how my idea of fun changed depending on which one I was around. One time, when I was about seventeen and had just got my license, m0y sister and I went to Robin's without telling my mother, and she came looking for us with Gram. When she found us (at Robin's house, predictably), she escorted us out of the house and told us to go home, me red-faced with embarrassment and frustration. I even had my car taken away from me for two days as a punishment.

Despite these questionable events, I liked hanging around with Robin, and, looking back now, I can see this was chiefly because she didn't treat me like I had any health problems, which was a rarity for me back then. Sadly, though, we lost touch with each other over the years because she went into the drugs scene, and I wasn't exactly wanting to put myself more at risk than I already was. I'd tried to talk Robin out of drugs, of course, but she'd retorted that I was "trying to run her life", so, inevitably, I abandoned my efforts, and that was the last time I spoke to her for years. So, maybe in the end Mom was right about Robin, but I still had fun with her while the friendship lasted, and that's what matters in life: good relationships and memories.

Years later, Robin and I did happen to meet up again, but it just wasn't the same. We both had kids (spoiler alert!) and totally different lives. We were parents, and very much so not teenagers anymore, and while that may sound like an overly obvious statement to make, it proved a very odd, even disorientating, moment. I can remember us talking in high school about what we thought our futures held as though it was yesterday, and I can even more vividly recall her envisioning our children playing together and us visiting each other in our own homes.

And now here we were, practically strangers in all the ways that mattered.

Robin, if you're reading this, I want to thank you for teaching me what the real world was like. I'll always remember the times we shared when we were trying to make it on our own in the most confusing time of our lives. I will always consider you a friend, even if we parted ways once upon a time.

Once Robin dropped out of school in the ninth grade, I was left no option but to go make new friends, and this led me to Kathy and Margaret.

Kathy was in the same grade as me, and we became friends on the very first day of high school, in English class (and, happily, we remained in the same English class throughout high school). Margaret, meanwhile, was one year behind us. Margaret and I shared geometry class together, and we liked geometry so much that we took it for two years, finally passing at the end of the second year. (We didn't really pay attention during the first year!)

Weirdly, our geometry teacher had this thing with frogs and talking in class: if he caught you talking, he'd throw a stuffed frog your way to get your attention. There was an assortment of frog sizes depending on whether or not this was a repeat crime: small for the first time, a little bigger for the next, a little bigger for the next, and then a *giant* frog that was probably about two to three feet tall for the fourth time. My sister was in the same class, and I can confirm she got a frog thrown at her several times. Though I was no saint; I got a couple thrown at me, too! And the first time Margaret got one thrown at her, she got scared and shrieked when it landed on her desk, which made me, and the entire class fall into hysterics.

Margaret and I also had our lunch break together, and I went to Margaret's house after school very often. Most of the time, though, the three of us hung out together, and during those precious high school years, my locker was the designated "community locker", where Margaret, Kathy, my sister and I would store all our belongings. This often meant there wasn't even any room for my own books, but I didn't mind. I relished these friendships, and locker space was a small sacrifice to make.

As I'm sure is the case for most people, it was also around this time (high school) that I started to notice guys more. Most of the boys were either my friends or afraid of asking me out because of my heart problems–that, or because of the fact that I had six older brothers and a father at home. I can imagine both were pretty intimidating. Health and scary brothers aside, though, it's likely I wouldn't have had a "real" boyfriend before this point anyway, since Mom wasn't exactly keen on me dating. Although she *did* let me go out with a neighbor's grandson, Kenny.

Kenny and I had known each other since we were little kids (he'd visit his grandparents, who were our neighbors, on every major holiday), and when he asked me out, both his grandmother and my mother approved of it. Obviously, the relationship didn't last long because he lived too far away (to my understanding, teenagers don't typically look for a long-distance gig), but this was no skin off my back. In fact, the brevity of the relationship was no shock to me whatsoever because after every date, Kenny would give me a kiss goodnight, and one hour later, like clockwork, I'd be vomiting in the bathroom.

Yes, *vomiting.*

It was the weirdest thing. And for the record, that never happened with anyone else I knew. It was clearly a Kenny thing, which is next level strange, considering he was a lovely kid, and I actually really liked him.

I never told Kenny I got sick after our dates (obviously; that would've been a pretty gigantic knock to the ego), and once he started working, he stopped visiting his grandparents so often, so the relationship (thankfully) reached an organic end. We remained friends, but there would be no more Kenny kisses for me, and that suited me just fine.

So yes, I suppose one could say that in the ways that counted, my dating life was pretty non-existent during my high school career. Until, that is, June 25, 1981. The summer before my senior year.

On this day, Kathy asked me to go to her friend Chris' house and hang out. "Sure, why not?" I shrugged.

When we pulled up, Kathy said, "There he is! Outside with his brother, sister, and father."

I raised my eyebrows. "I didn't know Chris was a guy."

"Oh, I guess I didn't mention that."

"Nope, you left that part out."

We parked across the street from his house, and both got out of the car, and with that, Kathy introduced me to Chris and his father, brother, and sister. Then, the three of us (Kathy, Chris and I) went to McDonald's, where Chris was working at the time. We were in the middle of our conversation when Kathy's father showed up. She headed out to see him, and Chris immediately followed to check she was alright.

While I sat there waiting for them to return, I thought, *How nice he is to go see if she's alright!* He'd also opened the door for us when we'd arrived and was very polite. What a gentleman!

After a few moments, they both returned, and we continued our conversation before heading back to Chris' house, where we again resumed our conversation before it was time for me and Kathy to go so, I could be home before my curfew.

He gave Kathy a kiss on the cheek goodbye, and I found myself wishing this was me.

"Goodbye," he said to me warmly. "Nice to meet you!"

I said the same, and we were off.

An innocent outing on the surface of it, but the cogs started turning, and a seed had been well and truly planted.

On our way home, Kathy and I got lost. I very rarely drove out of my town, and Chris lived about twenty minutes away, so this was like an epic voyage for me. I called my house, my grandmother's house, and my dad's garage numerous times, and no one answered. Growing desperate, Kathy called her house, and no one answered there, either (remember this was way before cell phones).

We finally found our way home, and when I finally arrived (and after my curfew), I had my mother, father, and grandmother waiting for me.

"Where were you? Why are you so late?" they immediately demanded.

I explained that I'd been to a friend's house with Kathy, that we'd gotten lost on the way home, and that I'd called a few times. My sister heard this commotion and, thankfully, interjected, "I'd just got to bed when heard the phone ring several times, but didn't get up to answer it."

Whew! I was out of the hotseat.

After all that, I was finally able to tell my sister about the guy I'd met.

About a month later, Kathy's sister called me and invited me to Kathy's surprise birthday party. I agreed, of course, and then asked, "Is Chris coming?"

"Yes—and he asked if you were coming, too."

Oh.

On the long-awaited day, I arrived at the party early and took a seat in the living room. I had a good view of the whole house there, and so when Chris came in, I could watch his every move unnoticed. From my vantage point, I watched him say hello to Jen before walking through the kitchen, down the hall, to the den, and then to the sitting room, looking as though he was searching for something or someone.

It was when he came back into the kitchen that he saw me, and, once he did, he made a beeline for me and re-introduced himself. After we exchanged greetings, he took a seat on the opposite side of the room. And then, throughout most of the party, we didn't speak a word to each other. It was only when they served the cake, and I went to the breakfast bar to grab a fork that we bumped into each other again. Chris was sitting in the kitchen, and when he saw me come in, he beamed.

As I reached for a fork, he started talking to me, and so I sat next to him... and just like that, we couldn't stop talking. During this conversation, he told me he was on a delayed entry program for the military and was due to start duty in October.

This felt like a sucker punch to the gut. *I finally meet a nice guy, and he's leaving,* I thought despondently.

As we were talking, I turned around about to put a piece of cake in my mouth, and he snapped a picture. "Kathy would be upset with me if I didn't get a picture of her best friend at her birthday party," he said teasingly.

I smiled and said, "Yeah, right! Good try."

He then placed the camera on the counter, and so I snatched it, turned around, and took a picture of him. "Kathy would be upset if I didn't take a picture of you at her birthday party."

We continued to talk for a while before I told him I had to go. He quickly said he needed to go, too, and since he'd parked behind my car, he asked if he could walk me out to my car.

Yes. Yes, yes, yes.

When we arrived, we talked a little while more before asking if we could go out sometime.

"Sure," was my simple, nonchalant answer.

With that, he gave me a kiss on the cheek, said, "I'll call you," and started walking away.

"Excuse me," I called to his back. "I don't mean to be forward, but you need my number to call me."

"Oh, yeah, that's right!" he said, laughing and flushing slightly, and turned back to my car. And so, I gave him my phone number and he gave me another kiss on the cheek and opened my car door for me. And just like that, we were dating.

I told my mother as soon as I got home that I had a date that Wednesday night. "But don't tell Kathy if she calls," I said firmly. "I want to tell her." I didn't know what kind of relationship Chris and Kathy had, after all, and if *they* were dating, I'd obviously cancel as quickly as I could. I was pretty sure Chris wouldn't have asked me out if he were seeing Kathy, but still, it paid to be cautious.

On the day of the date, I called Kathy and asked her to come over to talk, which she did. Once we were in my room, I told her, "I need to talk to you."

"What's up?"

I took a deep breath. "I have a date with Chris tonight..."

She gave me a hug and wished me luck.

Confused, I asked her, "Aren't you and Chris dating? If you are, I won't go."

She laughed. "Me and Chris are just friends. We grew up together. And I'm happy for you!"

I was relieved at this revelation, and, of course, I went on the date with Chris. And it was *amazing*.

After that night, we started seeing each other every Saturday and Wednesday night. Shortly after that first date, I went back to school as a senior (Chris had graduated in June), and so instead started seeing him every weekend. We only met up briefly during the week because of school. Plus, I still worked at the nursing home, so my free time was pretty limited.

I remember one evening when we were out, Chris was using his dad's car, and as we pulled up to a stop light, the horn started going off and *wouldn't stop.* I just sat there laughing as Chris desperately pounded the steering wheel. In the end, he had to get out of the car and pull something under the hood. I continued laughing even after the horn had stopped, and even today, when I think back to this, I can't help but start giggling.

For Chris' birthday that year we went to the amusement park in my hometown, and we made a full day of it. I *love* Ferris wheels–the bigger the better–so Chris and I went on the Ferris wheel... and got stuck at the top! I started swinging the car, laughing uncontrollably as Chris gripped the handrail with panic. "Stop!" he finally said, and I did. He said kiddingly, "Remind me to break up with you when we get back on the ground. I can't date someone that likes heights this much!"

I didn't, of course.

One week before Chris was due to go serve in the military, I was invited out with his family to dinner at a Polynesian restaurant. After the meal, there was a hula dance contest as entertainment, and Chris and his brother were chosen to go up on stage. Chris' parents and I laughed so hard we were crying: the guy up onstage instructed Chris and his brother to put a grass skirt on, and off they went. His mother said we should have taken pictures and sent them with Chris to bootcamp, and I couldn't agree more.

Basically, Chris and I had an incredible time together (when we could see each other), always laughing and talking and having fun... and then, before we knew it, the date of his departure was upon us. After bootcamp, Chris was then transferred to Vallejo, California, for his schooling, and, of course, it was time for me to return to school, too.

During this last year of school, Dr. Dick said I couldn't take gym class due to my heart condition, and always the stubborn and determined one, I promised him that if he let me participate, I'd stop if I got tired during the class. While he didn't seem too happy about this negotiation, he finally accepted, but had me promise again that if I got tired, I would definitely stop and rest.

I promised. I was so excited at the prospect of being able to take gym class for the first time ever that I think I would've promised *anything*.

With this news, my mom called the school, spoke with the principal, and let him know I would now be able to go to gym class, but that I had to stop and rest if or when I got tired. He agreed, and just like that, I was designated to a class—the same one, as it happened, that my sister and Margaret were in.

The first activity of my first class a few days later was volleyball, and, despite my enthusiasm, I didn't do very well; this was my first time ever playing it, after all! This wasn't helped by the fact that I quickly grew tired and told my gym teacher I had to sit down to rest.

She told me no.

I frowned. I reminded her about the agreement I'd made with my doctor, to which she responded, "If you sit down, you'll get a zero for the day."

My sister, overhearing this conversation, interjected, "Karen *must* sit down to rest."

"Don't interfere."

Feeling powerless (I did *not* want the zero), I went on playing, and, sure enough, I got very tired, was sick, and ended up in the ER that very same night. I told Mom what had happened, of course, my sister adding that she'd also tried to get the teacher to let me rest but that she wouldn't listen.

It was also while I was in the ER that Dr. Dick was called, and it's safe to say he was *not* happy to learn of the state I was in.

The next day, Mom went to the school *and* Dr. Dick called and spoke with the vice principal, the gym teacher, and my mom. Dr. Dick apparently said to the gym teacher and vice principal, "Karen *begged* me to take gym, and she promised me that she'd stop if she was tired."

"Both Karen and her sister told the gym teacher during class that Karen was tired, and you, the gym teacher, wouldn't let her sit down and rest, telling her that if she did, she'd get a zero for the day," my mom added.

"Well, a lot of kids say they're tired and want to get out of playing," the gym teacher hedged.

"With all due respect," Dr. Dick said, "Karen ended up in the ER last night because she overdid it and *wouldn't* have ended up there if you'd listened to her and her sister." He then informed them that he'd instructed the ER to send the medical bills to the school so they could foot it. "I'll still have Karen take gym class, but if this happens again, I'll be having your job, and you will not teach in Massachusetts again," he concluded firmly.

After that, Dr. Dick hung up the phone, and Mom picked up the baton. "If this happens again, this teacher"—pointing to the gym teacher— "will never teach again *anywhere.*"

Sure enough, the next time I was in gym class and needed to rest, the teacher told me to take a seat and resume playing whenever I was ready.

Had that really been so hard to say before?

From then on, gym class was nothing but fun, and I wasn't pressured to do the whole class if I didn't feel like I could. It's the small things in life!

Margaret and I attempted to play tennis during gym a few times, and it was very surprising if we managed to volley the ball even just a few times. But hey, baby steps, right? Would we be tennis pros? No. But boy, did we have fun! Watching us play tennis was like watching Lucy and Ethel; you had to laugh! At least we got an A for effort.

Years later, in my ceramics class, I made two female tennis players, named them Karen and Margaret, and sent them to Margaret. She laughed and said she loved them.

The weeks that preceded graduation were probably the best time I ever had in my life. I missed a lot of school during this time, and not (for once) because I was sick, but because pretty much all I had was study halls. What was so good about this, you ask? Well, Kathy worked in the office, so I could just tell her I had a doctor's appointment, and she'd give me a pass and I'd be permitted to leave school for a couple of hours! And if she and I happened to have study hall for the first class of the day, we'd go out to breakfast and then get back to school in time for our next class.

Genius, right?

During this time, Margaret also had her confirmation (she was Catholic), and her aunt from Ireland (her sponsor) couldn't get to the U.S. in time for it—so Margaret asked me to take her place. I was delighted and honored, and of course accepted.

After the ceremony, Margaret and I (along with her parents) went to Friendly's for a sundae, and when we all received our orders, Margaret asked, "Who wants my cherry?"—and, being a high schooler and having just returned from a confirmation (of all things), I had to really try not to laugh at the unintentional innuendo. I was doing well at holding my giggles in until her mother burst out laughing, which made *me* laugh, which made her *dad* laugh. Margaret's mother and I were laughing so hard we were physically crying. Margaret, meanwhile, had also started to laugh a little uncertainly, but didn't know what we'd found so funny. Later that evening, Margaret asked me about this, so I explained it to her and her face was the picture of shock. "My parents found *that* funny?" she echoed with horror.

Unfortunately, the following year, Margaret graduated from high school and moved back to Ireland. Gladly, though, I've visited her since she moved. (More on that later!)

A week before graduation, Kathy and I went out to breakfast with other friends of ours before school was due to start and had a particularly great time. Before we left, I stood on the hood of my car and yelled at the top of my lungs, "We're seniors!" to the traffic that was passing by. After that, everyone in the group started beeping their horns. It was awesome, and so exhilarating. I, quite literally, had the world at my feet, and I felt invincible.

Basically, my senior year went way too quickly. I enjoyed being in school, learning new things, having lunch with my friends, and just having fun—and we know what they say about time passing and having fun!

I am also lucky enough to say that my mom and dad threw me a graduation party, which was attended by friends and family. This was a surreal moment: I couldn't believe I'd made it to this point despite my heart problems and everything else that had been thrown into the mix. I felt that my simply still being here was a true accomplishment, which, in many ways, it was.

I also couldn't believe that I wasn't to be in school anymore. I was never going to be with my school friends day in and day out again. Most of us were going off to college in September and knew we would probably lose contact with one another throughout the years, and I knew I would deeply miss those school days. I still do, at times. They were the good old days; a turning point in my life.

Time doesn't stop for nostalgia, however! And so, sure enough, I graduated from high school in June 1982, and for my graduation gift from my parents, I received a ticket to CA for a three-week visit to Chris. This was my first trip away from home, and I travelled solo. And, unfortunately, for a short time, at least, it was a scary trip: I had a three-hour layover in Atlanta, which I partially spent walking around the airport, and at one point, I approached an employee and asked him where the game room was. He responded, "I'll take you myself."

I followed him to a stairway... and there, he tried to kiss me.

I put my hand on his chest, pushed him back against the banister, and said, "I don't think so. I'm going to see my boyfriend. Plus, I have older brothers who are bigger than you, and they could get here shortly. You don't want that."

My bluff seemed to have the desired effect: he got the message loud and clear, and instantly took off.

Extremely shaken (as an understatement), I went back out to the airport to where my plane was going to be and stayed there for the remainder of the wait time. I was shaking and crying and thinking to myself, *I don't like traveling alone.*

Mercifully, the rest of the trip went without a hitch, despite this very unfortunate introduction to solo travelling. As planned, I was in California with Chris for a total of three weeks. He took me to the beach, as well as many other places in the area, and while he was working, I explored the area on my own, either by foot or city bus. The day before I was due to return home, we went to San Francisco and explored the city, wandering the famous PIER 39 and Lombard Street. We had a great time, though we did get lost, which led to Chris getting frustrated. In the end, we pulled over and talked for a bit before continuing, and eventually found our way back to the hotel.

The next day, I left CA and Chris, but I wasn't leaving as the same person I'd arrived as: I felt like I'd matured so much in the three weeks I'd spent in CA and felt as though I could do anything. To this day, I believe that parents must send their children out into the world and allow them to make mistakes and learn from them. I'm glad that my parents let me go on that trip, even though I was really terrified on the way home due to what had happened on my way there.

Upon my return, Chris and I wrote to each other, and I prepared to go away to college.

It was also around this time (right before I left home for college) that I handed in my notice at the nursing home. I'd worked there for a total of two years by this point (from right after my sixteenth birthday to my high school graduation), and I'd learned a lot during those years, met many new people, made some good friends, and learned of how some seniors are, sadly, forgotten by their families. I also learned some history from the residents about what life was like when they were my age or younger, and I'm *incredibly* thankful for this experience. It had a very positive impact on my life, and I still think about some of the residents I took care of back then. It's funny how now, when I see a senior citizen with blue hair, it doesn't surprise me in the least!

Most importantly, though, I'm proud of the work I did there. I always took care of the residents the way I would have wanted someone to care for my parents, and I loved every minute of it.

So, my feet planted firmly back in my hometown and my time at the nursing home over, I prepared, mentally and physically, to go away to college at Fisher Jr. College in Boston, an all-girls two-year college (though today, it is a four-year coed college). It wasn't too far from my family, which meant I could come home for the weekends and holidays, and I was close to Boston Children's Hospital if I needed medical care.

I must admit that I was scared, but also massively looking forward to it. I was so ready to embrace the next chapter in my life.

6
ADULTING: NOT ALL IT'S CRACKED UP TO BE

Before we knew it, college move-in day had arrived, and Mom, Gram, and Chris (he was home on leave) helped me with the giant task of moving into my dorm. At first, I was assigned a room on the fifth floor in a building that had no elevator (obviously a no-no for my condition), so Mom, always my champion supporter, made a beeline for the registration department and asked for a room change. A few moments later, I heard my mom call at the foot of the stairs, "Karen!"

I hurried to the railing... and so did about fifteen other girls.

Mom tried again. "The one on the fifth floor!"

A chunk of the girls left, leaving three of us.

"Karen *Rosner*!"

Finally, I was the only one looking down.

"Your room change is in another building on the second floor, and the building has an elevator!"

So, with that, we moved all my stuff into the new dorm, and then Mom, Gram, and Chris were gone.

I sank onto the middle of the floor, boxes surrounding me, and started to cry. I was afraid of this sudden change. Would I like it here? Would I make friends? Would I do well in my classes? All these questions were rushing through my mind at a dizzying speed. Everything felt so alien and big and overwhelming.

Finally, I stopped crying and started to unpack the boxes. This took me the rest of the day. It was while I was doing this that I found an unexpected stowaway: Mrs. Beasley! I'd packed her away and stored her at home before setting off for college, finally accepting it was time to leave her behind... only it seemed Mom had snuck her into one of my boxes.

Admittedly, this put a smile on my face, despite all my anxiety.

Unpacking completely, I went to dinner and sat alone—the last and only time I was to do so for the rest of my college career.

After dinner, I finished unpacking and arranged my room. I "decorated" the top of my dresser with my medication bottles (the life of someone with a heart condition!), and it was as I was unpacking the many bottles that it fully sunk in that it was now *my* responsibility to take my medication properly. No more Mom poking her head around my door to check I'd taken it on time.

This initially filled me with anxiety, but then I thought, *I can do this*—and I was right, of course!

Room-unpacking and -arranging complete, I then explored the dorm and college buildings. It was when I was heading back to my room that I ran into a woman coming down the laundry room stairs. We said hello and started talking, and, when it became clear we were enjoying ourselves, I invited her to my room, where we continued to talk for a while. Her name was Sheryl, and she was a senior, which meant she could tell me about most of the professors and a girl I "had to meet", who was called Heather and was also a senior.

Sheryl left after an hour or so, and I instantly felt much better about being there, my worry quelled in the presence of my new friend. By the time I went to bed on that first night, I felt infinitely calmer than I had that afternoon while unpacking my boxes. I was filled with nothing but excitement as I thought of all the new experiences and adventures that were awaiting me.

The next day was registration for classes, so I met up with Sheryl in the hall, who brought me over to Heather. Heather was in the line for books in her wheelchair, and the first thing I immediately noticed was how tall she was, even when sitting down. She also had a cast on her foot. I asked her what had happened, and she explained that she'd broken her ankle in several places after falling on some cobblestones and that her doctor had had to reconstruct it. I nodded knowingly, and with that piece of new friend trivia out the way, Sheryl officially introduced us, and I wasted no time in inviting them back to my room that evening to talk. (I had a private room; plus, I was closer to the ground floor than they were, Heather being on the third and Sheryl being on the fifth.) And the rest is history: from that point, we became friends fast, glued to the hip. We'd all study together, take walks to the 7-Eleven a few blocks away as a study break, and spend pretty much every other free moment together.

Around one month after meeting her, I went up to Sheryl's room to find she wasn't making sense when she was talking to me. She appeared to be drunk, but I couldn't see any beer cans or alcohol bottles around. Shaken, I remembered that Heather had known Sheryl the year before, so I went to Heather's room and said, "Sheryl is acting drunk."

Heather ran past me (her cast was off at this point), up the stairs, and into Sheryl's room. She talked to Sheryl rapidly, went to her fridge, and gave her some apple juice. Oddly, a few minutes later, Sheryl started to make sense and wasn't acting drunk at all.

"What just happened...?" I asked, unnerved and confused.

Both Sheryl and Heather explained that Sheryl was diabetic and acted like that when her blood sugar was low. Turned out she'd just needed a drink of juice.

That was a quick (and worrying!) lesson, and my learning it meant I was able to help Sheryl throughout the year whenever it happened again.

Indeed, while some lessons I learned during that first year of college took place in the classroom, there were many that took place elsewhere. Basically, this whole period was a *huge* learning curve for me. I learned what a loyal friend is and what one will do for you; how the little things matter more than the big things; that opposites do attract, and don't always mean disaster. After all, Heather and I were opposites (mainly in the fact she came from an affluent background and I didn't), but when we became friends, none of that mattered. What mattered was that we enjoyed being around each other and that we valued our friendship. We were thick as thieves and had each other's backs through thick and thin.

In late October of that year, I became sick, and didn't get better for a long time. The college's doctor diagnosed me with mono, the flu, and Hepatitis non-A and non-B, which wasn't contagious, but just made me feel terrible. I was lucky to have the people I had around me during this time, as Heather immediately took up the role of looking after me in the period between my diagnosis and me being able to go home: she brought meals to my room, went to my professors to collect my assignments, and stayed by my side whenever she could. I was incredibly grateful to her during this time.

In the end, I had to go home for Thanksgiving break a week early to rest and get better, and, thankfully, I was well on the road to recovery after a week of rest. Thus, I stuck the rest of the semester out, though not with as much energy. As luck would have it, however, I then got pleurisy and ended up in the hospital for a couple of days, though a bonus of that time was the fact that I became friends with the college nurse, who I saw a minimum of once a week. Every cloud!

Once I was fully better, it was time to start preparing for finals. Heather, Sheryl and I constantly studied together, and the night before the last day of finals, Chris and the three of us gathered in my room for Chinese food, laughing and talking. We exchanged gifts and chattered away, like we always did, and while this was nice, it also had an undeniable undercurrent of sadness to it: we knew we soon wouldn't see each other for a few weeks. We were all looking forward to getting a break, of course, but were equally wondering what we were going to do at night now we couldn't walk down to 7-Eleven on Charles Street as a trio.

In my mind's eye, I can still see clear as day me, Heather, and Sheryl sitting on my bed smiling and laughing that evening. Chris took a picture of us while we were sat like this, and we've each got a copy of it, which I'm thankful for. It is a memory I still treasure.

We said goodbye to each other the following day, after finals. It was sad, and we all cried lots, but then we looked on the bright side and reasoned it was just a few more weeks until we'd be back together again. And, sure enough, right after our break, we resumed our old routine of going to classes, studying together, and walking down to the 7-Eleven on Charles Street. The only change to our routine during that semester occurred when Sheryl's sister, who had a condo a few blocks from the college, asked us to watch the house while she went to Florida for a month. We were able to order groceries and put it on Sheryl's sister's bill, which was really great, and the condo had a fireplace, two bedrooms, a kitchen, and a living room. We were trying to save on heat, however, so the three of us slept on the sofa bed. It was cozy, to say the least, and, naturally, I got relegated to the middle.

We had a routine where before going to bed, we'd check the door was locked and that the burners on the stove and all the lights were off–and one night, when it was my turn to do the checking and I was in the kitchen to see if the stove was off, I yelled out so Heather and Sheryl could hear me, "On, off, off, on, on."

With that, I turned off the light and went to bed. A few moments later, Heather said, confused, "Rosner, the stove is on and you're coming to *bed*?"

"Yeah. There's nothing next to the stove to cause a fire."

With that, I turned over and tried to go to sleep.

Heather, clearly concerned, dashed into the kitchen... to find all the burners and the oven were off.

Sheryl and I were laughing. "Got you!" I said to Heather when she returned to the room.

She didn't think it was very funny.

Still laughing, I asked her, "Do you *really* think I would leave any of them on?"

"I guess not," she admitted–and then finally started to laugh.

The next day, Heather got me back. I was lying in bed while the others were cleaning the apartment when Heather said, "Come on, Rosner, get out of bed and help us."

"I will," I said groggily, and then turned over, trying to go back to sleep. Then, Heather came over and started folding the sofa bed up while I was still in it. Sheryl stood at the side, laughing hysterically. "Come here!" I squealed to Heather–and, when she obliged, I grasped for her shirt... but she moved closer than I expected, so I accidentally slapped her in the face instead.

She and I were both stunned at this.

She finally let me out of the sofa, and we apologized to each other... and swiftly went back to cleaning the apartment.

Today, she still insists I slapped her in the face, to which I say, "Well, you folded me into the couch!" and we both dissolve into giggles.

A few weeks into that second semester, a new student named Elaine arrived, and she soon became one of us: we ate together, studied together, and walked to 7-Eleven together. Elaine was a lot like me in the fact that she was street smart. Because of this, we'd often tell each other jokes Heather and Sheryl would never get—though they did get us one time...

Sheryl, Elaine and I were in my room looking at a *Playgirl* magazine when I got a phone call (remember this was the eighties: no cellphones. Just payphones in the hall) and had to leave the room to take it. When I returned, my door was locked and they wouldn't let me in, though I could clearly hear whispering and giggling. I had a feeling they were up to no good, and when they finally let me in, I left the door open because it was so hot in the dorm. They kept telling me to shut the door, however, saying they had to tell me something that no one else could hear. So, I shut my door and immediately noticed on the back of the door a picture from the *Playgirl* magazine with a caption above it that said, *Oh, Roz!*

Up to no good, as I'd suspected.

We started to laugh, and struck with a new idea, I called Heather down to my room, who we repeated the prank with. The look on her face was hilarious! Then, we all looked through the magazine, Heather at one point asking, "Is he circumcised?"

"This is Anatomy 101 class!" we laughed.

I still have that picture they hung on my door, and when I look at it, I remember that day with a big smile—an unlikely piece of memorabilia from my college days!

The school year ended quickly (probably thanks to these antics!), with Heather and Sheryl due to graduate that year. Elaine and I went to the ceremony, and it was great seeing them, and our other friends get their degrees. It was a proud moment, to say the least, and one I'll never forget.

Heather had a dinner at The Ritz-Carlton after the ceremony, which her parents invited me to, and that was really nice, too. The Ritz is a very classy restaurant in Boston, and we had a really good time, Heather glowing all the while.

After the meal, we walked back to the dorm, where my mother and grandmother were both waiting for me. With that, we packed up my room and then went home, Heather, Sheryl, and Elaine all doing the same. We made promises to keep in touch over the summer and throughout the years... and, well, we did stay in touch for a few years. Heather and I were bridesmaids in Sheryl's wedding that summer, which was very nice. I wish the others stayed in touch, too, but it's difficult to do so when you have your own families to take care of. Regardless, I still think of these people as my dear friends, and always will. They became my soul sisters during our time together at Fisher, and that's not something you can change just because we're no longer in regular contact. On the contrary, they still have a very special place in my heart, and they always will.

In the summer of 1983, I went back to CA, and when Chris completed his tour there, we drove across the country from Vallejo, CA, to Easton, PA. On our trip, we saw the Grand Canyon, the Gateway Arch, the meteor crater (just a big hole in the ground), Universal Studios, and even the Hollywood sign. The trip took us nine days in total, and was amazing, though very hot: it was the middle of August, and we were driving through the desert. Undeterred, we made sure we stayed hydrated and proceeded to have an amazing time. It was incredibly interesting to see all the places I'd heard about on TV.

That was my first trip across the country, though I've done a few more since then, and I saw different things each time–things that made me appreciate our country more and more.

When we arrived in PA, I moved in with Chris' mother, which suited us fine, since we never saw each other because of our conflicting schedules. (Not that there would have been a problem if our schedules *had* corresponded, and we saw each other often. It was just convenient that I didn't feel as though I was intruding too much!) I also lived with her rent-free in lieu of me caring for Amy (Chris' little sister) while she worked, which was very kind of Chris' mother, and certainly worked for me: Amy and I had fun, and really made this time our own. I still see and fully acknowledge how blessed I was to not have to pay for anything at the time.

Taking advantage of this privilege and freedom, I took a course at Allentown College (now DeSales University) in my spare time.

It was a year or so after this move that Chris and I started living together in Virginia Beach, VA. This, for me, was a huge learning curve, since I'd always lived either with parents (whether mine or his) who took care of the household bills for us or in college. Now, however, it was Chris and I handling all the standard adult responsibilities that come with living independently, and the sudden change was more than a little bewildering. Yet, of course, we adapted, and now, we were embarking on our new life together. Our first apartment was three blocks away from the beach, which was great, as it meant I could either go for a walk or ride my bike across the coast each morning before work. Chris and I were also in the habit of walking the strip in the evening.

And yet not all was as happy and romantic as it probably seemed. Chris and I were working different shifts (I was still working as a nurse's aide), so we often went days passing each other by—and, like most couples, Chris and I had our arguments, though we worked most of them out. I believe these were just the normal growing pains of a relationship and moving in together, although admittedly, sometimes our conflicts were a little more serious than that. There was a time when I moved out of our apartment and rented a room from a family member because I'd found out Chris had cheated on me. I started dating a friend of mine and Chris' for a few months, adamant that Chris and I were not getting back together, but, in the end, we ended up having a very long conversation and deciding to get back together. (Believe it or not, Chris and I are still friends with the guy I dated. I actually introduced him to a friend of mine, and they completely hit it off, got married, and had a daughter. Weird how life works out sometimes!)

By the time we got back together, our lease was up, so we had to move to another apartment—only now, Chris was on base more due to his job. So, *I* rented a new apartment and he just stayed with me whenever he was off duty, which was quickly becoming less and less frequent.

This was certainly not the life or routine I'd envisioned, but this was what I had signed up for... Right?

One evening in December 1985, Chris and I were having dinner when I suddenly became short of breath, my heart pounding fast. I initially refused to go to the hospital, but Chris, concerned, insisted on taking me to the emergency room of Norfolk General Hospital. My heart was going at approximately one hundred and twenty BPM, and I was having trouble breathing—and no medicine was helping.

I had an intern come in to tell me what I was feeling was not heart related.

"The hell it's not," I snapped. "I feel my heart beating as if wants to get out."

Clearly a little frazzled by this response, they called a cardiologist, who couldn't understand what was happening. I explained that I had a congenital heart condition, five open-heart surgeries, and a history of atrial flutter, and he admitted me to the Children's Hospital of Norfolk for the night.

The next day, a doctor came into my room, who somehow already knew who I was *and* all of my history.

"How do you know all this?" I asked him.

"I used to care for you when you were a baby at Boston Children's Hospital," he smiled.

I knew in that moment that I was in good hands. I was very happy to finally have a doctor who actually knew what was happening to me.

He asked me if I wanted a pacemaker.

"Yes!" I said. "I've been asking for one for years, but the doctors said I didn't need it then."

"Well," he said, "I can get you a pacemaker, but I can't do it here because of your heart arrythmias. I'd need a dual chamber pacemaker." (Dual chamber pacemakers were new, and only certain hospitals/doctors knew how to put one in and how they worked.) "You'll have to go to South Carolina. The doctor there is from Boston Children's Hospital, too."

I was eager to get this process started and was accordingly sent down to South Carolina a couple of days later by bus.

Yes, *bus.*

This was probably the longest bus ride I ever took. Halfway through the trip, I felt so unwell and out of it that I was ready to ask the driver to pull over and call an ambulance to take me the rest of the way.

In the end, sweating, disoriented, and exhausted, I finally got to the Medical University of South Carolina, admitted myself, and went up to my room, promptly falling asleep at around 3PM and only waking up when my mother arrived the next day, at around noon. I then signed the papers and had surgery the very next day. No messing around here; I meant business! Before that, though, I went down to see the doctor who was going to perform the surgery, to find there was a kid in the same room who was about four years old. He said, very cheerfully, "They're going to put something in my belly to make my heart work right!"

I smiled. "They're going to do that to me, too."

He beamed.

If this kid isn't scared, I shouldn't be, I thought to myself–and, sure enough, I wasn't after that.

So, on December 12, 1985, I got my first pacemaker.

The surgery went well, but my left arm and shoulder were very sore afterwards. I was also told I couldn't go home until I could put my left hand on top of my head. In the meantime, my mother had to feed me, which felt acutely embarrassing for a twenty-two-year-old. (In case you didn't get the memo yet, I'm a lefty.)

The day before I went home, the surgeon came in with some med students and told me they were going to check the pacemaker over the telephone every three months. He also reeled off everything I couldn't do: karate, shooting a gun from the left side, wrestling, etc. I asked him if I could play the piano.

"Sure, why not?"

"Because I didn't know how to before the surgery."

He and the students laughed. (I still don't know how to play the piano.)

He put a halter monitor on me for the day and had it read before I went home the next day, when the cardiologist tech came in to take the monitor off... and then told me I'd have to keep it on because the doctor forgot to turn it on. Great.

Chris called every night while I was in hospital, and I was finally discharged on December 21. I did fine for a few weeks; it wasn't until after New Year that I started having problems again. A veteran recognizing these symptoms by now, I booked an appointment with my cardiologist in Norfolk that my friend, Kim, accompanied me to. We planned to go out for lunch after it.

We never made it to lunch that day.

I told the doctor that I was experiencing palpitations, and he did an echocardiogram, to find that my heart was out of rhythm again and one of the wires from my pacemaker had disconnected from my heart. This meant I had to go back down to South Carolina to get it fixed immediately. This time, however, Chris and I had a little more money (courtesy of Christmas), so I flew down to South Carolina instead of bussing it.

Thank God. I think I would've lost my soul if I'd had to do another one of those bus journeys while feeling so unwell!

During this visit, the surgeon went back "in" and reconnected the wire to my heart, and after the surgery, I asked the doctor if he'd screwed the lead in a couple extra times so it definitely wouldn't come undone again. He gave me a small smile and said he had.

Thankfully, I was able to leave the hospital the day after the surgery, and I didn't have any other issues with the pacemaker for a while.

Yet the end of the stress was not yet in sight.

Chris was by this point back out on a tour, and I was out of work due to these hospitalizations. The kicker was, I wasn't *allowed* to go back to work until at least six weeks after my first surgery, and I'd almost been at the six-week point when I'd had to go for the second surgery—so that meant *another* six weeks out of work.

This meant I was facing eviction from my apartment because I had no money for rent or food.

I applied for state aid and received heating assistance and food stamps, but I couldn't get help for the rent. So, I reached a point where I had to think, *Well, I'll have food, and whoever has this apartment can have heat.*

My phone was turned off, and I was behind on my car payments. It's definitely fair to say that financially, I was in hard times. But I didn't give up. I looked for options, and I found them. I talked to a guy at the bank and told him what was going on, and he told me he'd help me in any way he could. I paid twenty dollars a month on my car just as a goodwill gesture (my regular payments were one hundred and nineteen dollars a month), and I went to the welfare office to see if I could get any assistance with paying my rent—yet the only help women could get was those who had children. Accordingly, the woman there suggested that I write to my boyfriend and ask him to send me some money or call my mother and ask her to help. However, I'd already promised myself I wouldn't go back to my parents for any financial help once I'd moved out, and I'd kept that promise so far (though I know my parents would have helped if I'd asked). So, instead, I told this woman, "By the time he'd receive the letter and send one back, I'd be homeless." I knew Chris would have helped if he'd been around, but the only way for us to communicate at that time was by writing letters, and this matter was far too time sensitive for that.

Stuck between a rock and a hard place, I, in desperation, got a lawyer from legal aid, who helped me to stay in my apartment by negotiating with the company which owned my apartment building. He told them that I'd pay as soon as I got my first paycheck and then would pay every week after that until I was up to date with the rent.

In the end, I went back to work at the nursing home one week before Chris came home and, indeed, started paying the rent back. To show my gratitude, I also told the man at the bank that once I was fully up to date with my rent, I'd start paying him more, too. He said not to worry, however, and that he knew I was trying and keeping him abreast of the situation.

When Chris came home, he paid the outstanding amount required to get me fully caught up on the rent, from which point I started paying more toward my car.

I was at work one day shortly after this when I got a call from the bank manager; he was calling to discuss my delinquent account. I told him I could make up the payments soon, and asked if I could meet him the following day to discuss a plan to get up to date with the car payments. He agreed to this plan... and then I woke up the next day to find my car was gone.

I called the police, and they said the bank had repossessed it.

I was furious.

When I got to work, I called the bank and spoke to the manager, who said the person who'd been helping me keep my car had been transferred to another branch because he'd been "helping me too much". I told him that the other guy knew my situation and that was why he'd been helping me: because I'd been keeping him informed of what was going on, and he knew it wasn't my fault. "I'm coming in today to discuss it with you," I concluded.

"Sure, you can still come in."

So, after work, Chris took me to the bank, and I marched straight into the manager's office and proceeded to yell at him. "How am I supposed to pay the money back if I don't have a car to get to and from work? I expect you to come to my house at six-thirty in the morning to take me to work and then be there at three-thirty to pick me up!"

"I can't do that," the man said warily.

"You also said you weren't going to do anything until I came in today!" I pressed on. "And you *lied* because you had it towed this morning! So, thanks a lot for all your help—and I feel bad for Bob, because he was trying to *help* someone, and he has *you* as a boss, who punished him by transferring him to another branch."

With that, I stormed out of his office. I could vaguely hear him saying something in response, so I just turned to him, said, "I can't believe *anything* you say because you're a *liar*," and slammed his door as hard as I could on the way out.

The whole situation was *very* frustrating, especially considering I was really trying to pay my bills. The manager was clearly only thinking of money and not the person or situation, unlike the representative who'd been helping me before he was transferred. Don't get me wrong, I totally got that it was business, but jeez, talk about a lack of empathy!

Looking back now, it seems very possible to me that this event was (subconsciously, at least) the catalyst for me opening my non-profit later on, which helps people who've just had transplants and then find themselves in these situations. I fully believed (and still do believe) that companies should try their utmost to put the customer before the sale, and this belief was really driven home to me as I walked out of that bank that day.

As I was leaving, I said to Chris, who'd been sitting in the waiting area, "Are you coming or not?"

He just got up and followed me out, mute.

The (other) positive side of this event is that the repossession never showed up on my credit report—a blessing, since I owed much more than the car was worth. I honestly think the radio in the car was worth more than the car itself by that point!

I wanted, and was willing, to pay my bills, but when you don't (and, at least temporarily, can't) have an income, suddenly, everything changes. I was (thankfully) able to get back on my feet financially soon thereafter, but God, was it a ride while I was on it. One thing was for certain: financial stress was not to be underestimated, and especially not the financial stress straight out of hospital. I, and everyone else in the same or a similar position to me, deserved more. More support. More understanding. More grace. And I knew that one day, I would do my utmost to make that a reality for others.

7
THE NORTHERN WEDDING

Chris and I worked well together in a crisis, but soon after the crisis was over, Chris went back to his "old ways": I found out he was seeing another girl behind my back, and this time, I told him to stay on the ship and not come back.

His way of showing his remorse was to then ask my closest friend at the time out–who, of course, said no.

This meant Chris and I separated for about a month... until he came over and said he had a question.

"I may have an answer," I said sarcastically.

"Will you marry me?"

I froze.

In a daze, I walked over to the couch, and said, "What?"

"Will you marry me?"

I just sat on the couch in shock. My head was saying "yes", but the words, "I must think about it," came out instead.

"Okay," he said. And then, "For a week?"

"I need more than a week." I had to think about what Chris had put me through. But I did love him, and I *did* want to be with him. It'd be remiss for me to not mention that I was also young and naïve, and thought that once we were married, he wouldn't cheat. *Really* naïve thinking, obviously, but hey, love is blind, right?

That night, we went out for dinner to Ships Cabin Restaurant in Norfolk, which had the best seafood. There, I had lobster for the first time in my life. I remember the waitress asking me if I wanted boiled lobster or lazy man lobster, explaining boiled lobster was when you had to crack it open and dig the meat out yourself, whereas lazy man lobster was when the chef cracked open the body, exposing the meat within. I told the waitress I'd have the lazy man lobster tonight, and when she left our table, Chris said, "Smooth move."

I just smiled at him.

After dinner, we went to see Sam Kinson (a comedian who was just kickstarting his career) on the college campus, and then went home. In other words, it was a nice but normal night. It was as though perhaps the biggest question I'd ever been asked *wasn't* weighing on my mind.

In the end, it only took me two weeks to come back with an answer to his question—and of course, that answer was yes.

I was happy with this at the time, wrapped up in my excitement, but looking back now, I know I should have said no, understood that he'd never change, and started with someone new (or just stayed on my own for a while). But, again, I was young and naïve about relationships (especially *my* relationship) at the time. So, instead, we spent our time talking about getting married. We didn't have a date set (we had to get a license and everything else), but we did know we were going to get married by the justice of the peace before having a bigger wedding in Massachusetts with our families during the summer, when he could take leave.

I was overjoyed at the thought of getting married and fulfilling my dream of spending the rest of my life with Chris. Everything seemed to be falling into place.

Or did it?

Chris and I finally got married on May 6, 1986.

Chris had had duty the day before, so I picked him up from the ship on

Tuesday (our wedding day) at around 3PM, both of us still in our work uniforms, and took him to the city hall to get a marriage license. Then, we went upstairs to the justice of the peace, where we performed the ceremony. (Before this, however, Chris had to go back to his car to put more quarters in the meter. The whole affair was very well-planned and romantic from start to finish, clearly.)

The ceremony itself was short, but nice. I had a lot of trouble getting the ring on Chris' finger when I was supposed to and I was barely able to say my vows, both because I was so nervous (a sign, maybe?), but I got through it. All the while, I was thinking to myself, *This is a huge step I'm taking.*

In truth, I was afraid, but I suppose most people are afraid of the unknown.

After the ceremony, Chris dropped me off at work two minutes late, where I immediately told my colleagues I'd just got married. I didn't have any proof of this because Chris had the paperwork, and I didn't have my ring on (it was being sized). Even still, my boss said I could go home early if I finished my work. So, I finished my work at eight forty-five—a whopping fifteen minutes early. (They really rolled out the red carpet!) I then had the weekend off, but Chris had duty.

We were in that routine for a few weeks.

The next day I had off, I called the Department of Social Services and informed my case worker that I'd gotten married, meaning they could close my case. I didn't need food stamps and public aid once I married Chris; we were able to make it on both our incomes. I felt good knowing that I could get off public aid, though I also felt secure in the knowledge that it would still be there for me if I ever needed it again. I believe public aid should be used for those going through hard times, but not as a permanent solution for years on end. Plus, I felt embarrassed and like everyone was looking at me when I used food stamps. Back in the eighties, food stamps came in a booklet and were like coupons with a dollar amount on them—not like today, where there is a discreet debit card that would never give away the fact that that you're on food stamps.

Chris bought me a Subaru BRAT for a wedding gift since I (still) needed a car, and I loved that truck; it lasted for a good for a few years.

We finally went on our honeymoon on Memorial Day weekend: camping in Jamaica, VA. It was a nice campground, and they had outside church services on Sundays. We went to the lake and went hiking, and generally enjoyed each other's company. Chris had a difficult time starting a campfire the first night, but after that, it was smooth sailing!

We returned from our honeymoon on the Sunday, so we unpacked everything and relaxed on the Monday (Memorial Day)—and by the Tuesday, we were thrust back into reality with the realization that we'd forgotten to set an alarm the night before and that Chris had to be on the ship in fifteen minutes.

We both jumped out of bed in a huge panic.

He got in the shower while I called the ship and spoke to the person on-duty. We were lucky it was our friend, Sam, who I explained the situation to and told Chris would be there as soon as he could. Sam said (of course needing to keep things professional) to tell Chris he needed to be there by eight (what would've been an hour late) at the latest. Then, on a more personal note, he said, "Karen, you marry him and take him away for a honeymoon, and now, he's coming in late! Boy, you're changing him!"

I reassured him that Chris would be there by eight—which, thankfully, he was—and he didn't even get into any trouble or receive any extra duty. Newlywed luck indeed!

My point is, while getting married had felt like a huge decision and step in our lives, it actually had very little impact on our daily lives. We both went to work, both continued with our conflicting schedules, and I'm sure, both remained unsatisfied with various aspects of our relationship. It was an amicable and harmonious partnership, but was it what I'd always dreamed of? What *had he* always dreamed of? No. Almost certainly not. I wasn't on my "path", so to speak, and that was to become increasingly obvious over the coming years.

Chris and I decided to have our proper wedding in Massachusetts on August 31, 1986 (ten days after his birthday and ten days before mine). We had the day planned to the T: we were going to have it at Forest Park Garden with the priest from my church, and I was about to order invitations and look for my dress when Chris called me at work one day and told me he was going on a cruise.

"No problem," I said brightly.

"The cruise is going to be June sixth until October sixteenth."

"Yep, sure, no problem."

It wasn't until Chris repeated the dates that I realized: August 31 was right in the middle of that time period.

It clicked.

A pregnant pause ensued.

"No wonder you're calling me from the ship," I said quietly. "You don't have the guts to tell me in person."

"That's right," was all he said in response.

Umm, what?

So, as probably goes without saying, we had to cancel all the plans for the wedding.

I was deeply disappointed. I'd been looking forward to celebrating with our family and friends, but it seemed the Navy had another plan.

Want to know the irony of this? The cruise was called the "Northern Wedding".

While Chris was off on this cruise, I moved us into our new apartment completely alone—though the move was from a furnished apartment to another furnished apartment, which I suppose helped things. I had a friend give me moral support, though she couldn't help me physically because she had a cast on one of her legs. Nonetheless, I successfully moved all the boxes into the new apartment, and then I picked her up from work so she could help unpack things while I put them away.

Except picking her up from work turned out to be more interesting and much less straightforward than I thought it would be.

I remember this as if it was yesterday: I was driving on the highway on a Friday afternoon at 5PM, listening to the radio (specifically, the song *Working for the Weekend* by Loverboy) when I passed a car from the middle lane.

I guess the driver didn't like this, so he cut in front of me before slowing down.

I then proceeded to pass him again, pulling in front of him, and he retaliated by following me all the way to my friend's work. I stopped to pick up Calla (my friend), and as she was getting into the truck, I noticed this man was walking over to us. Panicked, I hissed at Calla, "Hurry up! He's coming to my car!"

"Who? Who?" she asked, alarmed.

"The guy from the highway."

I started to take off before Calla even had the door closed. It was only when I'd already started to drive off and I saw the guy run back to his car that I realized, with an instant feeling of horror, that he was a police officer. (It later turned out that he'd been in his uniform but in his own car because he'd been on his way to work, hence why I hadn't realized straight away.)

"Oh, damn, he's a *cop.*"

I stopped, and the guy came up to my window and (weirdly) said, "I'm not going to kiss your ass!" three times. He then asked for my license and registration.

Now, in VA, you have a city registration and a state registration, and I always got them mixed up because they looked exactly the same: the only difference was one said "city" and the other said "state". So, I handed him my license and (erroneously) my city registration.

He huffed, "I want your *state* registration, not city," and threw the city registration back at me.

Aggressive much?

I sheepishly handed him my state registration.

"You can pick these up at the precinct."

Odd.

Thankfully, Calla knew how to get to the precinct, so she directed me, and when I headed inside to retrieve my license, the officer had a complaint for me to sign stating that I had a) been speeding and b) been disorderly toward and used foul language to a cop.

I scanned the contract with something close to amusement, and said to the officer, "What will happen if I don't sign it?"

"You'll spend the night in jail."

I thought about this for a moment and then said, "I could use the rest, but I have my friend in the car." And with that, I signed it, and Calla and I were on our way.

We first went to my old apartment to make sure I'd gotten everything out. It was when I was walking through the place that Calla suggested I check the closet. Good thing she did, because there were all our clothes!

A few days later, I was to appear in court for the charges brought against me by the police officer. I told the girls at work what had happened, and they said he was a jerk and had probably had a fight with his wife that he was taking out on me. Regardless, I went to court, as ordered, and had to listen to him the entire time. They didn't even let me say anything.

The charges were reduced to disorderly conduct to a police officer, and I told the judge I wanted to appeal it. So, I filed the paperwork to do just that and scheduled another court date.

When Chris returned from his cruise, I filled him in on what had happened since he'd left, and he said he was proud of me for not letting some cop walk all over me. He then leaned back and said, "There's never a dull moment with you, is there?"

I mean, he wasn't wrong.

I didn't hire a lawyer for this case, though I subpoenaed Calla to court so she could get paid for the time missed.

Soon enough, my court date arrived, and Calla and I were against the police officer and the district attorney. The judge had the officer take the stand first, and the district attorney asked him a ream of questions. First: how fast was I going when he passed me?

"She was going between fifty-six and fifty-seven miles per hour."

Did he pass me?

"Yes. When I got in front of her, I could tell she was swearing at me." He then stated that I'd said "motherfucker", and that when I'd passed him, I'd had my middle finger of my right hand plastered against the passenger window.

Then, the district attorney asked Calla to take the stand.

What had she seen and heard?

"Once I got in the truck, Karen told me he was coming to her car. When the officer approached her car, he stated that he 'wasn't going to kiss her ass' three times. He then made her drive without her license and registration." (Later, I asked Calla if she'd ever heard me curse, or even say the word the officer was claiming I had. She said that she'd never heard me curse, instead stating that when I get upset, I usually say "shoot" or "fudge". Further testimony to the fact that the police officer's claims were a total fabrication.)

It was then that I was asked to take the stand, from which point the district attorney asked me questions regarding what had happened on the highway before

I stopped to get Calla.

"I was singing along to Loverboy's song *Working for the Weekend.* It was playing on the radio when the officer pulled in front of me, when he stated he read my lips by looking at his rearview mirror. He slowed down and I passed him, and then he followed me. When I stopped, I saw him get out of his car and didn't realize he was a cop, and so started to take off. When I saw him going back to his car in my side-mirror, however, I realized he was a cop and stopped. He came up to my window and started swearing. I hadn't known he was a cop at first because he was in his own car." I paused. "If I'd been going between fifty-six and fifty-seven miles per hour and the speed limit was fifty-five, he must have been going faster in order to pass me. The officer has also stated I had my middle finger of my right hand plastered to the passenger window, but if that was true, I'd have had to lean over to reach the passenger window–and then I would have turned the steering wheel and caused an accident."

In the end, the judge agreed with my version of events and dismissed the case, without me having to pay any fines. Once this verdict was read, I looked over to the police officer and district attorney, and it's safe to say he didn't seem very happy–unsurprising, considering he and his district attorney had just lost the case!

I was very happy at this result, and, encouraged, I proceeded to file a formal complaint against the officer at the police station and write to the editor of the local paper about what had happened. I was later informed that the police officer had been suspended from the force for two weeks without pay immediately after the complaint and article to the editor came to print, which made me very happy to hear: I felt good knowing I hadn't let this guy walk all over me; that I'd shown I wasn't afraid of him just because of his title. It was also good knowing that I could take care of myself, even when the situation at hand was an intimidating one.

I'd decided to file the complaint and write to the editor because I felt this cop had taken advantage of his power and position. He even had me break the law by making me drive without my license and registration. I also learned from a friend back then that this cop was somewhat known for taking his anger out on women in this way when he'd had an argument with his wife–so turned out my colleagues' hunch had been right! Only that day, he'd taken his anger out on the wrong woman.

I just hope he changed his ways after our time in court.

After the court case was over, Chris and I fell back into our routine: he had duty every three days, and I worked my various shifts.

When Chris initially returned from his latest cruise, I admittedly had to readjust to having him around, though he still largely wasn't present due to his cruises and duty days. Perhaps due to this new period of reorientation and lack of purpose, I found myself deliberating what to specialize in at college. I was doing well at pre-med and wanted to apply to medical school, but my cardiologist at the time informed me that this wouldn't be good for my health or heart condition due to the hours required.

I listened to my doctors, of course, and discussed my conundrum with Chris, who suggested I become a social worker.

"I don't want to take kids away from their parents," I objected.

Chris was persistent, however, and suggested I go to Norfolk State University (our local college) to speak with someone in the social work department with an open mind. "Do it for me," he persisted.

So, I agreed to both requests: that I visit, and that I do so with an open mind.

Chris had duty the next day and I had to work in the afternoon, so I visited the college the following morning. There, I spoke with the dean of social work, who explained the different areas in which a social worker could specialize, including policies, research, substance abuse, child welfare, and medical environments. Sufficiently intrigued, I signed up for classes that day for the following fall semester, and when Chris came home the next day, he asked me if I'd visited the college.

"I did."

"What did you think?"

I grinned. "I'll let you know after my first semester."

He was thrilled.

In the end, I spent eighteen months at Norfolk State before transferring to Anna Maria College to finish my bachelor's degree in social work. During my final year at Anna Maria, I completed an internship at the local Department of Social Services agencies (an *incredible* experience, by the way), and as I was leaving for my first day of my internship, Chris gave a me a kiss goodbye and said, "Remember, we can't afford nor do we have the room for all the children you'll want to rescue."

"Got it."

My first task was a visit to the home of a sixteen-month-old baby who had a diaper probably as heavy as he was and a bruise just below his right eye. The mother told us he'd gotten this bruise from falling near the coffee table and hitting the corner, yet the father said it had happened when he'd put the baby in the crib, which had (allegedly) fallen apart as soon as he'd placed the baby in it.

A likely story.

While the supervisor and I were talking with the parents, I put the baby on the table in front of me, swinging his little hands back and forth and making him do a little twist from his torso, and he started laughing with delight. Clearly, the baby wasn't getting much attention from his parents.

As my supervisor and I stood to leave, the baby grabbed onto my ankle. My supervisor told me to pick the baby up and give it to the mother, and, of course, I obeyed, yet there were tears pricking my eyes as I walked away, ignoring the baby crying as we walked down the stairs. This was very, very difficult to do; every instinct in me was telling me to run back and take care of that baby myself.

I knew then why Chris had said what he had before I'd left for the day.

That baby was subsequently put in hospital for a few days, and he gained five pounds during his stay—and yet when he went back home, he started losing weight again. The baby was thus removed from the home on the grounds of child neglect.

I felt so bad for him.

Perhaps unsurprisingly, however, there were many other cases like that, and I felt like I helped the kids as much as I could, even if my heart did break a little every time, I had to walk out the door.

Shortly after I went back to school to complete my social work degree at Norfolk, we got the news that Chris' ship was going to the Persian Gulf. This was June 1987, a tough time to be going there: it was just after the *USS Stark* had been hit, which had resulted in the deaths of many sailors. So, naturally, this news wasn't massively welcomed—by me or the other Navy wives. I knew this because during his other cruises, I'd gone to the Wives Club meetings and met the other wives whose husbands were on the same ship. There were five of us that hung around with each other: Ellen, Trish, Kim, Pam, and me. Ellen had just adopted a child when we met, while Trish was pregnant with her first child, Kim had a four-year-old, and Pam had three children and was pregnant with another.

Meanwhile, I was married, in school, and childless.

In other words, I wasn't your typical Navy wife: I was going to school, working, and paying the bills for us. Chris would get the allotment, and I would get the paycheck, and in the Navy, that didn't happen much. Usually, the man was in control of everything, and the women were there to bring up the children.

Anyhow, I digress.

On June 6, 1987, Chris and all the other sailors of *USS Kidd* left for the Persian Gulf. There were reporters all over the dock, and as the ship was departing, a reporter came up to me and asked me how I was feeling. I said, very sarcastically, "I'm so happy that my husband is going to the Persian Gulf that I'm crying."

Trish had to calm me down. I then turned to the reporter and said, "If anything happens to this ship while they're over there, more than three hundred and fifty wives will want answers for why the *USS Kidd* was chosen for that mission."

"What did you and your husband discuss last night?" the reporter pressed on.

"We discussed insurance and how to cash it in, if needed."

A relatively long interview, clearly—yet the only thing that made it to the paper was the thing about the insurance. Obviously. You gotta love journalism.

During that cruise, which lasted six months, a lot happened. First, I fell at a local Kmart store and messed up my knee. It happened like this:

Trish's dad was visiting her at the time, so the three of us went out shopping. Trish was six months pregnant, and as she and I were walking down an aisle, chatting away, I suddenly realized I was on the floor. Turned out I'd slipped in some spilled soda that was all over the aisle. Thankfully, Trish had only stepped in the sticky part of it.

Trish went to grab the manager, who figured out that one of the cans in a six-pack of Coke cans on the aisle had a hole in the bottom of it.

By that point, my right knee had swelled to twice its normal size, and the manager quickly insisted that Kmart would take care of any medical bills.

"If you do, I won't sue," I responded simply.

Trish's dad kindly carried me out of the Kmart, into a restaurant (to get some food), and to the hospital. There, I was told that I'd sprained my knee and that I had to stay off it for a couple of days.

The following day, my knee hurt even worse, so I went back to the hospital and was given an appointment with a knee specialist, who thought it best to enroll me in physical rehab. That didn't help much, however; I'd barely start walking before my knee gave out. Yet somehow, I continued to go to school, work, and rehab for some months. A sprained knee wasn't going to stop me!

In November, I had knee surgery and sued Kmart because they in fact didn't pay a dime of my medical bills, which resulted in me accumulating ninety-day past-due notices.

It ended up taking me three years to get anything from Kmart.

The silver lining of this was that my knee surgery was probably one of my most minor surgeries to date: it was only a one-day surgery, though I was out of it all that day and the next day, too.

The second notable thing that happened while Chris was away went as follows: the routine we (us wives) had with our husbands was that whenever they hit a port during their cruise, the guys would call home. Trish, Pam, and Kim's husbands all had the same days off, and so they usually all received their calls at the same time, whereas mine and Ellen's husbands had a different day off.

Well, the ship hit a port, and was scheduled to remain there for three days, and all of us received a call... all of us except Pam. And even by the time the ship had gone back out to sea, Pam's husband *still* hadn't called, so she (naturally) grew worried about him. Trish and I felt really bad as we watched Pam grow more and more distressed, and so, wanting to take the matter into our own hands and help our friend to feel better, we sent her husband, Bill, a telegram stating that Pam was worried, and please could he call at his next port call? I signed my name on it and thought that would be the end of it. (As we were about to find out, Trish and I could be like Lucy and Ethel with our ideas: we thought they'd make everything better, but most of the time, they'd just make more of a mess!)

A few days later, the ship settled at a port, and Chris called me to see what was going on because he, Bill, and David (Ellen's husband) had all been called to the Executive Officer's office. The EXO had handed Bill the telegram from me and Trish and demanded to know what was happening. Apparently, Bill had been really busy at the last port call and so hadn't had time to call home, and, upon receiving the telegram, the Executive Officer had warned the men that they "should have more control over their wives". Chris had responded to this by saying, "Excuse me, Sir, but I don't have control over my wife when I'm home, so how am I supposed to have control of her when I'm halfway across the world?"

To this, the EXO told them to communicate more with their wives and warned them that if this happened again, they'd get extra duty. He even told them they could lose a stripe, should this (or something similar) reoccur.

I was proud of how Chris had handled the situation, though I didn't understand why a) David had gotten in trouble when his name hadn't even been mentioned in the telegram and b) the husbands were instructed to "control their wives". No one has control over me, and no one ever will. I understand it was the military (which, of course, has its own unique culture and standards), but my point still stands I did things *my* way, even if that sometimes got me in trouble. Not wanting to make things harder for Chris, however, I did decide to lay low for a while; I didn't want his career to suffer. And distractions there were: on October 1, 1987, Trish gave birth to her baby.

As soon as she went into labor, Trish called me to let me know she was going to the hospital in Portsmouth, VA, and that I should meet her there. So, I headed over after work... and got stuck in the Portsmouth tunnel due to after-work traffic. Ellen, Pam and I had warned Trish not to go into labor on a Friday afternoon and/or payday, but, of course, she didn't listen, and so off she went to the hospital on a Friday at 3PM, when most of the military was getting off duty *and* it was payday.

I was getting increasingly stressed over the traffic still being at a standstill when I looked out of the window and saw a rainbow. I relaxed a little after that; I felt like it was a sign that everything was going to be alright. And it was: I got to the hospital in plenty of time.

I went in to see Trish, who was hooked up to a fetal monitor and having contractions around every eight to ten minutes. As I watched the monitor, I realized she had a contraction whenever it went up to eighty-nine, at which point she'd started screaming, squeezing my hand.

I discovered that day she was really strong. I'm surprised I left with my hand intact.

"Come on, that was only a fifteen. You can do better than that!" I joked at one point.

"Fuck you."

In case you were unsure, Trish hated pain, and didn't have much tolerance for it.

She also kept asking for Pam and Kim, and I kept telling her they were on their way; that they'd be here soon.

"That's what you said an hour ago, and they're still not here!" she hissed.

It was then that I realized there was a big clock on the wall behind me that Trish could see. Oops. "Well, if you'd listened to us and not gone into labor on a Friday at five, we'd all be here," I joked feebly.

A little later, she asked for some pain relief. When the nurse came in to give it to her, he asked, "Are you allergic to any medicine?"

"Just give me the fucking medicine and ask questions later!"

I fought a smile. "No, she's not allergic to any medicine," I told the nurse. "She's not very good with pain. She's not usually like this."

I must admit it was a little funny seeing Trish act this way.

When Kim and Pam finally arrived, she was a little calmer, and a few hours later, Trish gave birth to a beautiful baby boy. He was flirting with us as soon as he came out: the nurse wheeled him to the nursery and stopped so we could see him, and we could see him winking at us.

That little baby is now thirty-five years old. Time flies when you have a kid!

For weeks I helped Trish with the baby, mostly keeping him in my arms, and a few weeks later, Dan got to come home early from the Persian Gulf cruise to be with his family. Everything wasn't as rosy as it seemed, however: Trish and Dan were planning on getting a divorce and had only been waiting for Dan's return from the cruise to initiate it.

Things were cordial enough for a few days after he came home... and then things got really bad: when they were at court to finalize the separation agreement, Dan physically took the baby from Trish's arms and ran. Trish, horrified, called me as soon as she got home, and we immediately started searching for the baby. Watch out, Cagney and Lacey: here come Karen and Trish!

We called all over before finally going to the source and talking to one of Dan's friends to see where he was. While Trish was talking to him, I called Dan's sister in Illinois, and, to my surprise and joy, she fessed up on the call. She at first said, "He called me a while ago, but he didn't tell me where he was," but quickly changed her tune when I told her that if she didn't tell me where he was, she could get in trouble for helping him, and that she may go to jail, too. After that, she hastily said, "He and Mom just called me from his apartment."

I hung up the phone and ran to get Trish and tell her what I'd learned.

With that, we went back to the apartment to check whether he was there. And, of course, he was. So, we went to a corner store and called the police, who escorted us to the apartment so we could get the baby. The police told Trish not to say anything to Dan; just to grab the baby and his stuff and leave.

When Dan opened the door, we could see his mom holding the baby. The police officer instructed her to give the baby and diaper bag to Trish. Trish started to say something when I quickly cut in with, "Trish, don't," and, with baby in arms, we got in my car and went to Ellen's, where Trish and the baby would be staying.

What a *ride.*

Many of my social work skills that I had learned came in handy that day. As a matter of fact, I shared that story on my application to a program for social work in MS, and got in with that alone!

After that, Dan took off, and Trish hasn't seen him since that day. Talk about domestic dramas.

Shortly thereafter, I received news that Chris was coming home early because his stay in the Navy was coming to an end. I was so nervous the day he was expected home (which just shows how rare it was that he was at home now) that I called Trish about four times in an hour and asked her if she could do my hair. She said she would and told me to call her whenever I was ready for her to come over, so I took a shower, shaved my legs, put on my makeup, and called Trish to tell her I was ready.

I headed into the bathroom to start blow-drying my hair when suddenly, before I knew what was happening, Chris was standing there, asking me why I hadn't answered the phone.

I jumped out my skin and screamed.

Before I could say anything coherent, he walked out. I wheeled out of the bathroom in his wake, but he was gone. I almost wondered if I'd imagined the encounter, yet there he was when I went to the front door, hauling his bags out of a car.

I picked up the phone again, Trish still on the other end of the line. Sounding somewhere between bemused and alarmed, she said, "I guess you don't need me to come over, then?"

"No, thanks. Bye," I said in shock, and put the phone down.

I turned around, and there was Chris, carrying his bags with an annoyed look on his face.

"What are you doing here?" I asked him. (He hadn't been due home for another few hours yet.)

"Thanks for the greeting," he said testily. "I got a ride instead of taking the bus, which cut two hours off my trip."

I finally gave him a hug, and was slowly calming down from my scare, happy to see him but also dimly aware of the fact that even here, in his arms and in our home, I almost felt as though he was a stranger. He'd been gone for five and a half months. That wasn't to remain the case for long, however: he was on leave for a couple of weeks, and after that, he was going to leave the Navy.

Honestly, it felt great getting out of the Navy. It meant Chris and I were able to start planning for a family and life together without the constant interruption (or threat of constant interruption) of him going out to sea. Plus, being a Navy wife had been very difficult, primarily because I didn't much enjoy him being away. I felt as though our marriage stopped and started every time he went on a cruise. Of course, I understood that Chris had signed up for the Navy before he'd met me, and so I'd known full well what I was getting into when I entered a relationship with Chris. Plus, Chris' Navy career definitely made us both grow up fast: I became more responsible for myself and learned to be more independent. So, every cloud!

Regardless, I wasn't exactly unhappy to close on this chapter in our life, and I hoped that now, we would have enough time and flexibility to really tend to our life and relationship. Maybe we'd even finally be happy.

8

THEY TOLD ME I COULDN'T. THAT'S WHY I DID.

Chris and I moved back to MA in December 1987, where we both found jobs we enjoyed (I was working for a daycare while continuing to go to school). We were just getting settled into our new apartment when I started getting sick on Christmas day. I initially thought this was because of my job (I thought my immune system was going to have to get used to the kids coming in with colds, the flu, and other viruses) and so I got on some antibiotics from December until March and carried on.

It was only when I was visiting a doctor at a clinic around March that it came to light that my heart was swelling up. My doctor, finding this concerning, referred me to a cardiologist, who I saw the next day. His name was Dr. Haffajee, and when he asked me what was going on, I told him I'd had knee surgery in November and started getting sick around Christmas with strep, bronchitis, and other colds and viruses. I also told him that whenever I stopped taking antibiotics, I fell sick again around five to seven days later.

He told me to stop taking the medicine, come back to the ER to have some blood cultures done in twenty-four hours' time, and then wait for his call.

I did what he said and went to have the blood test the following morning. Then, Chris and I went to work and to a goodbye party for one of Chris' co-workers, and when we finally got home at around 10PM, we found a message on our answering machine asking me to call the ER. When I did, they said I had to come in and be admitted to hospital immediately because I had a blood infection known as bacterial endocarditis (a bacterial infection that attacks the heart). So, of course, I went straight to the ER, where I was admitted and given IV antibiotics. I had to remain in hospital to keep being administered these antibiotics for the next six weeks.

At first, this wasn't so bad because I felt very ill, but when I started to feel better, I struggled with the stay. I was only able to get a pass to leave the hospital for a few hours at a time, and I had major cabin fever. I also experienced something very upsetting while in hospital that really didn't help with my general mood: while my brother-in-law was paying me a visit, a nurse came into my room and said, "Are you going to stop using drugs?"

"Excuse me?" I said, bewildered.

She repeated the question.

"Have you read my chart?" I asked.

"I've seen your diagnosis and age, and concluded you were an IV drug user."

I mean, yes, while in hospital, I'd had a lot of IVs so they could get rid of my infection, but I'd never used IV drugs outside the hospital–*recreationally*, that is.

"Can you please get your supervisor for me and come back to my room?" I asked, trying to keep my cool.

She obliged, and when she returned with her supervisor in tow, I asked the nurse to repeat her question.

"Are you an IV drug user?" she asked.

"Where did you get that idea?"

"I saw your diagnosis and your age, and that's how people get the infection you have."

"Did you read my chart?"

"No; I just saw your diagnosis and age."

I turned to the nursing supervisor. "Please get this nurse out of my room and not have her come back." Before she left, I told the nurse, "If you'd taken the time to read my chart, you would have learned that I had knee surgery about six weeks ago and they didn't give me antibiotics during or after the surgery. I've also had a heart condition since I was born, so next time, read the patient's chart and never assume why your patient is under your care."

It felt as though this nurse was stereotyping me because of my age and condition, which isn't the correct mode of conduct in any situation. I should mention this hospital was one where a lot of medical students went on placement, but I was still very upset at how she'd stereotyped me, as was my brother-in-law, so I hope she learned an important lesson that day!

When these six weeks were finally up, I was more than ready to go home. Chris visited the day before I was due to leave with some flowers, which only added to my excitement. That night, however (the night before I was due to go home), I got up to go to the bathroom, and when I got there, I felt my heart pounding, and I started shaking. I tried walking back to bed but didn't make it. I fainted, and woke up on the floor.

I was *soaked* with sweat.

I managed to get myself to my bed and ring for the nurse, who, when she came in, called for the doctor. Turned out I'd had an(other) episode of atrial flutter. The doctor explained I might have to stay for a little while longer to control the flutter, which, of course, filled me with dismay. He then came in the next morning and confirmed what he'd said the night before: I couldn't go home because they had to take me off my medicine and start me with a new one.

I was then in hospital for another week.

I finally got out of the hospital on my anniversary. My doctor also gave me a note just in case I got stopped by the police explaining I wasn't an intravenous drug user but was having IV medication therapy due to a blood infection. (The doctor didn't want to put a central line in because it could also cause an infection.)

Once I was released from hospital, I couldn't go back to my job straight away (which my employer thankfully understood), and school was out until the summer sessions began, anyway, so I spent my summer completing all my courses from the previous semester so that when I started in the fall again, I wasn't behind. I did end up having to take one extra class, but that wasn't so bad, since I was taking five classes at the time. It could have been a lot worse!

In the end, I finished my coursework on time, though I also had to complete my internship during the summer on top of everything else. This meant I was due to receive my degree the following May. I then got my first social work job one month after finishing my internship (in August), at an agency for teenagers, which proved to be a very interesting role that massively propelled my professional development.

Meanwhile, on a more personal front, Chris and I had been trying to get pregnant for a couple of years by this point and were very close to giving up. My doctors didn't seem too optimistic, either, which was a bit of a kick in the teeth. My cardiologist had previously said that if I ever *did* become pregnant, it would be very dangerous, and I'd have to be watched very carefully.

At that time, Dr. Haffajee and I made a deal that if I got pregnant, he would get me through the pregnancy and after the birth I would have my tubes cut, burned, and tied.

After trying for two years (with no success), I finally went to a fertility specialist, who told me that I wouldn't ever be able to get pregnant due to my anatomy: in the past, I'd had ovarian cysts, and my uterus was tilted too far back. I accepted this (though not without a pang of heartache), and Chris and I accordingly decided that we'd adopt a child at some point soon.

It was around this time, in August 1989, that I went to Chicago to visit Trish and what was then her two-year-old son, who stuck with me most of the time. I noticed during this trip that there seemed to be something a little weird going on with my menstrual cycle (I had a strange period that lasted a couple of days), but didn't think much of it. I then went away to Boston for a weekend to meet up with my college friends Heather, Sheryl, and Elaine (yes, *the* Heather, Sheryl, and Elaine!).

When I returned home from my trip, I found Chris had organized a small birthday party for me, for which one of our friends made his famous pizza, and I was delighted. Yet there was something a little off with me: usually, I'd eat two or three slices of this pizza, but on that day, I felt like I was going to be sick just from looking at it.

It was then that it crossed my mind that I might be pregnant, but the thought quickly went out of my head. The doctors and fertility specialist I'd seen had made it abundantly clear that that was closer to impossible than it was unlikely.

During that weekend, I had a couple of glasses of wine, and about a week after my birthday, I became really sick, stuck on the couch for a week. I was vomiting, had the sweats... the works. I went to see the doctor, and he said, "Oh, I've seen a hundred million of these and treated half as many. It's a virus. Go home and rest–and take Tylenol for the fever."

So, I did what he said.

One week later, Chris and I were getting dressed when he said, "It looks like you're pregnant."

"Yeah, right. You know I can't get pregnant," I scoffed.

In October 1989, however, I went to see my cardiologist, who asked me how I was doing. I told him that I felt like shit. He asked if I could be more descriptive, and so I said, "Yes: I'm always tired, I have a lot of headaches, and I get sick every now and then, especially when I drink milk. I feel run down. I guess it's taking me a while to get over the virus I had last month."

"I'll tell you what to do: go home, take a pregnancy test on Sunday, and call me on Monday to let me know you're pregnant." He grinned.

"I *can't* be pregnant," I responded. "I was told I couldn't *get* pregnant."

Nevertheless, I went home and told Chris (who had just started his bachelor's degree) what the doctor had said. A seed of hope had been planted within me, and I couldn't help but share the conversation I'd had with someone. I wanted to allow myself to fantasize about the prospect of me being pregnant, even just for a moment and even if I didn't fully believe it.

That Saturday night, Chris and I had some friends over for dinner, and I refused the wine. Everyone looked at me in confusion, and so I shrugged and said, "I might be pregnant. I'm taking a test tomorrow."

They were happy, and I allowed myself, if momentarily, to hope for a positive test.

So, the morning of October 29, 1989, I took a pregnancy test–and, after waiting five minutes (the longest five minutes of my life!), I looked at it... and right there was the confirmation that I was pregnant.

I yelled, "Yes!" and started jumping up and down. I was so incredibly happy; that was the happiest moment of my life, in fact. Without question. I was ecstatic.

I hurried to show Chris the stick and said, "See! We're pregnant! The bottom line is blue!"

I think he was more in shock than he was excited about having a baby, yet I was still jumping up and down, beyond thrilled and unable to contain my excitement, smiling and yelling, "I'm pregnant!"

"You may not live through the excitement of this, never mind the pregnancy!" Chris laughed.

"I'll live through both! Watch!"

With that, I called everyone we knew, and received mixed responses: some happy; some worried; some, weirdly, angry. Among these phone calls was one to Barbara, who lived across the street and was really thrilled for me. Then, I called our friends who had been over for dinner the night before, and they were equally happy for me. Next was Kathie and Gopa (Chris' parents), and as soon as she picked up the phone, Kathie said, "I was just about to call you and ask what you guys want for Christmas!"

"Well, I have an early Christmas gift for you and Gopa. I'm pregnant!"

There was nothing but silence down the line for a few moments (she was crying with happiness and conveying the news to Gopa) and then we talked for about forty-five minutes. Just before we hung up, she said, "Oh! How do you feel?"

"Great! But please don't tell Amy; just have her call me. I want to tell her."

"Of course."

I then called my mother—the toughest call of them all.

"How did that happen?" was my mother's first response to the news.

"Mom, you've had eight kids. You should know how it happened."

"Well, if anything happens to you during the pregnancy, I'll never forgive Chris."

Clearly, she blamed him.

"You know, Mom, I kinda had something to do with it, too."

Even still, Mom wasn't too happy about the pregnancy, and I could understand this, to some degree. Her daughter, who she had fought so hard to keep alive, was now willingly endangering herself. And she wasn't alone in her feelings: most of my other friends felt a little mixed about the whole thing. They were happy because they knew how badly and for how long I'd wanted to be pregnant, but on the other hand, they had very real concerns over how on earth I'd survive a pregnancy when my heart condition was so volatile and unpredictable. I reassured them all that I would get through this like I'd got through everything else in my life, however. And, of course, that Monday, I called Dr. Haffajee and told him that I was, indeed, pregnant.

He answered by saying, "Well, this will be the easiest part of the pregnancy!"

"Yeah, but there's a problem. My OB-GYN doctor has left the area."

"In that case, I want you to go my OB-GYN."

"You have an OB-GYN...?"

He laughed. "My *wife's* OB-GYN, I mean."

So, I called the doctor, Dr. Hunter, and was able to get an appointment for November 8, 1989. During that appointment, he did an exam and told me I was sixteen weeks pregnant.

"That can't be. I was in Chicago without my husband during that time."

So, he scheduled an ultrasound for the following week and discovered that actually, I was just entering my fifteenth week, which meant I'd gotten pregnant after I'd returned from Chicago. He then gave me a prescription for prenatal vitamins to take daily and instructed me to come see him again in one month. After that, he wanted me to see him every two weeks from thereon out, since my heart was starting to give me some problems.

I remember that during my first trimester, I was very tired. I worked for a counseling agency at the time and my office had a couch, and so during my lunch hour, I'd eat my lunch and take a nap, asking the secretary to wake me after thirty minutes.

Of course, I told my boss I was pregnant as soon as I found out, and also gave him ample warning that I may have to take maternity leave early because of my heart condition.

One of my most distinct memories from my pregnancy was feeling the baby kick for the first time. It was such a lovely moment. It was after dinner, as I was doing the dishes, leaning against the sink, that I felt a very distinct kick, as if the baby was telling me I was leaning too hard. I called Chris, and he was able to feel it, too. This was such a magical moment.

It was when I entered my sixth month and was gaining more weight that I started having some problems: my heart would fall out of rhythm and start going extremely fast every so often. I spoke to Dr. Haffajee daily so we could adjust my medication in accordance with these complications, and every time he increased my intake so we could better control my heart, he told me he "didn't know how the medicine would affect the baby".

"I know. I understand," I said, unfazed. I had an unwavering belief that the baby and I would be fine.

My heart got worse the more weight I gained, however, and on February 23, 1990, Chris had to physically carry me to the couch because walking tired me out so much. I called in sick at work that day, and as I was buttoning up my robe after putting the phone down, I noticed my heart was racing (and was showing no signs of slowing down) and that I was suddenly very short of breath. Meanwhile, Chris was getting ready to leave for school, and somehow, from the other end of the apartment, he heard me gasping for air. He rushed to the living room and asked if he should call Dr. Haffajee, and I nodded yes, and proceeded to slowly give him the number. (In that moment, I wished he remembered phone numbers like I did. Saying each digit was getting more and more challenging with each passing second.)

We waited about five minutes for him to call back before I gave up and told him to just call 911.

In the end, the paramedics got me stable and took me to the hospital, from which point I was under the doctors' constant care. My heart was meanwhile going between one hundred and twenty and one hundred and fifty beats per minute, and my blood pressure was forty, meaning the baby wasn't getting much blood. For this reason, I had to be cardioverted in the emergency room.

I remember looking at Chris and telling him to call my mother. He promised he would, his eyes wide with fear.

What felt like two but was actually about ten minutes later, I opened my eyes. I turned to Chris and said, "Make sure you do call my mother," and he said, "I already did." I'd clearly lost all sense of time and place.

After I was stable, I was admitted to the hospital in the CCU to be monitored. At one point, I asked one of the doctors when I could go home, and he said, "When you become a mother!"

"But I'll get bored!"

"Well, I'll sleep better at night knowing you'll merely be bored in bed as opposed to the alternative."

When I was admitted to the CCU (Cardiac Care Unit), I had nurses from the UMASS Memorial Hospital labor and delivery unit "babysit" me over the weekend. They had a crash cart outside my bedroom door just in case I went into preterm labor, and I had the baby monitor on all weekend. After that, I was transferred to UMASS Memorial Hospital so they could continue to monitor my pregnancy and heart. Initially, I went to the CCU for a couple of days, and then I was moved to the cardiac floor. I was placed in the same room as a lady who was in her late eighties, and the smell of the food her family brought in made me feel incredibly nauseous (almost certainly a symptom of my pregnancy). My doctor came in at one point and told me he was going to keep me in that room for a couple of days, to which I responded, "I want to be moved to the antepartum and postpartum floor tomorrow, or I'll go home and stay in bed there."

"You can't go home, ma'am."

"Well, I can't stay in this room any longer."

In my mind, the options where he find me a room on the antepartum and postpartum floor, or I go home the next day. My mother had brought me up teaching me I was to stand up for myself in all circumstances, and as a social worker, I advocated for others all day every day—so now, it was time for me to advocate for myself. I had nothing at all against my roommate, of course; I just truly couldn't stand the smells.

"Okay, I'll find you a room and move you tomorrow," my doctor sighed.

This discussion took place on Tuesday evening, and once it had concluded, I laid back in bed, pleased—and, sure enough, the next day, I was moved to the antepartum and postpartum floor, where I had a private room but a lot of visitors.

As the weeks went on, I started having more trouble: I was gaining more weight and having more difficulty breathing, and just a few days after arriving in my new room, I went into preterm labor. I was contracting for six hours, and during these contractions, my breathing got even worse. I was on six liters of oxygen, yet I was still turning blue and having trouble breathing. The nurse called Chris to give him an update on my condition, and he told her to call him if they needed him.

Before the contractions got bad, Trish called me, and as they worsened, I screamed in her ear. Kiddingly, I told her it was payback from three years before, when she'd been having her baby.

"No fair! I can't see the monitor to see how strong the contractions are coming," Trish laughed.

She had to hang up eventually, but it felt nice having that company for a while, even if it just consisted of me screaming down the phone.

My nurse (who was also called Karen) was extraordinary that night: she stayed with me throughout the whole thing, and she let me squeeze her hand and distracted me with questions about my plans for the baby when the pain got terrible. I simultaneously had a doctor come in to check whether I was still not dilated, and it was when he arrived for his third check that I was starting to get agitated—from both the labor and the constant assessments. He still had his fingers in me, feeling for my uterus, when he said, "Just turn on your left side, and the labor should ease up."

"If you get your *fingers* out of me, I can do that."

Clearly, he didn't yet have the "bedside manners" encouraged in hospitals: he was an intern, and thought he knew more than he did.

That was the last time that doctor touched me.

After the labor subsided, I was able to get some much-needed sleep. As a matter of fact, I slept all the way until the following afternoon. After that, my heart got worse, and I was having difficulty just getting up and going to the bathroom: my heart would begin to race out of control until I got back into bed and rested for a while.

On March 7 (nine weeks before my due date), my doctor came into my room and asked me what I was doing the next day.

"Just lying around and getting ready to have a baby, I guess."

"Nope!"

I frowned. "I'm going home?"

"Nope!" He paused. "I think it would be a good time to have a baby!"

"I don't think so..."

"Why not?"

"It's nine weeks too soon."

"Wrong again!"

I was surprised. "Why so soon?"

"Your heart is becoming more stressed, and so the baby is becoming stressed. Plus, I don't want you going into preterm labor again during the night, when no one is around."

I nodded slowly. "Okay, fine."

And with that, I called Chris to ask him what he was doing tomorrow.

"I have errands and stuff."

"Well, *I'm* going to have the baby."

Naturally, he was very surprised and worried, and said he was going to go to the doctor's office to talk with him and see why it had to be so soon.

When he came to visit me that day, he was more nervous than I'd ever seen him before... and, amusingly, he was willing to do *anything* for me so he could stay busy and keep the nerves at bay. This was Heaven for a heavily pregnant woman: I saw on TV a commercial for caramel apples, and said, "Ooh, I could go for one of those," and—*voilà*!—a couple of hours later, there was Chris with homemade caramel apples! Then, I wanted a big plate of spaghetti, and Chris went straight home, made a batch of spaghetti, and brought it to me a little while later. Then, I wanted an ice cream sundae from Friendly's, and—say it with me!—he went straight out to get the sundae.

At one point, friends of ours, Mike and Donna, came to visit me. Shortly after their arrival, I managed to get Donna close to my bedside, and I whispered to her, "Get him out of here. He's driving me crazy."

She told Mike, and Mike, by the grace of God, managed to get him out of the room. From that point, Donna and I talked for a while by ourselves, and I told her how excited and nervous I was about having my baby so early.

Mike and Chris returned shortly after, and then Mike and Donna left along with Chris, who needed to go home so he could grab some things for the morning. (He was staying the night at the hospital with me.) Upon his return, he wedged a cot in the room and immediately fell sleep.

Men.

I, on the other hand, couldn't sleep. The nurse had previously given me something to help me nod off, but it didn't work; I was too anxious. My mind kept thinking about being a mom and what I would do, since I had nothing prepared for the baby's arrival. My baby shower was scheduled for the following Sunday. I wasn't worried about the labor itself or my baby or me surviving; I was just worried about these practical things, as well as how small the baby was going to be, being born so early. The doctor from the Neonatal Intensive Care Unit (NICU) had already talked to me about what they might have to do for my baby after it was born, including putting him on a respirator to help him breathe and having him live in an incubator for a while. He also told me that the baby may not survive.

"There'll be two patients after my labor, not one," I promised him. I knew and felt that my baby and I would be alright.

And we were.

9
MOMMY RUNS ON BATTERIES

On Thursday March 8, 1990, at 8:25AM, I gave birth to my son.

My mother and sister came to the hospital early so they could see me before I went down to the operating room (I was scheduled to have a C-section), and, as I was wheeled down, Chris was by my side. I was very nervous up until the point where the doctors gave me something to calm me down. I remember that my arm felt like it was burning when they administered the medicine; the last thing I remember is yelling, "My arm hurts!"—and then I opened my eyes and I heard a doctor saying, "Congratulations, you're a mother!"

"Oh!"

"Honey, it's a boy!" I heard Chris say.

"My stomach hurts," I murmured. (Remember, they'd not only done a C-section, but had cut, burned, and tied my tubes so I wouldn't get pregnant again.)

"Would you like some more pain medication, Karen?" I distantly heard one of the nurses ask.

Yes. A thousand times yes.

When I got to the recovery room, I asked how my baby was, and Chris told me they'd had to bring him up to the NICU.

I was in a lot of pain. I looked at Chris and said, "I'm glad we can't do this again." I then added, "I want to name our son Eric Christopher."

His face brightened at that. He nodded in agreement.

I love the name Eric and have since I was nine years old, when I read about a little boy in the newspaper called Eric. At that moment, I said to myself, "My first boy will be named Eric." And so now, I have an Eric of my own.

After this, Chris went to see Eric in the NICU while I waited to go back upstairs to my room, back to the CCU, so I could be closely watched for a couple of days. When I got upstairs, I asked for a phone so I could call some friends, and shortly after this, Mike and Donna came in to visit me, bringing a basket for me filled with baby stuff. They said they'd seen Eric from the window. My mother and sister also came by to see how I was doing, and during this visit, my mom showed me a picture of my new baby.

I fell in love with him in that instant. I couldn't believe he was mine.

I still hadn't seen him in person yet (one of the last, it seemed!), but for now, Chris came up to my room with another picture of him, and I put that picture on my nightstand, where it stayed until I left the hospital.

I still carry that picture around with me to this day to remind me of how fragile life is, and how lucky I was (and am) to have my son, Eric.

My heart swelled with adoration for this gorgeous little human. And it still does.

Ever since delivering Eric the day before, I'd been begging the nurses to let me see him, and it was while my nurse and Chris were finally getting me ready to pay my long-awaited visit to Eric that another nurse came into my room and told me that one of my brothers was here to visit me.

"Which brother?"

"Bruce."

Chris turned to me and frowned. "I know you have a lot of brothers, but I don't remember a Bruce."

"Me neither," I laughed uneasily.

It was then that Bruce walked into my room, and my eyes widened with shock.

"He's not my brother," I said to the nurse. "He's, my boss." I then turned to Bruce and said, "I want you out of my room."

Thankfully, the nurse was on the case, too. "Sir, you need to leave."

Bruce ignored us both, however, and continued to walk toward my bed. Chris went over to stop him and warned him to leave now, or he'd get security.

"I just want to know when she'll be back at work," Bruce finally said.

"Not today," I responded, incredulous. "Now get out."

Turned out Bruce had signed in as my brother because I was still in the ICU and only family could visit ICU patients. I was very upset at this, as an understatement. It felt as though my privacy had been violated at a moment when I'd been especially vulnerable, physically and emotionally. Not to mention the fact that this had delayed my visit to Eric, something I hadn't stopped thinking about and had looked forward to for days.

But the wait turned out to be worth it.

When I got out of that bed for the first time, I was in a *lot* of pain, yet that somehow seemed completely irrelevant from the moment I was wheeled into the NICU and laid my eyes on Eric for the first time. He was so small, weighing three pounds and ten ounces, and he was sixteen and a half inches long. He was lying on his stomach, and I was wheeled around so I could see his face. He had one eye open, looking right at me. It looked like he was saying, "So, *you're* the one who carried me for the last seven months!"

I couldn't hold him just then, but I could put my hand in the incubator and touch him. He was so wrinkled, and had downy hair all over.

When I looked at Eric and then at Chris, I told Chris, "This is what you're going to look like when you're an old man."

Chris didn't appreciate that comment, but it was true! Eric looked (and still looks) like his double.

Eric was on a respirator, like the doctors had told me he would be, though the good news was that he was only on the respirator for a total of four days in the end; then, he was just in the incubator, and was able to leave that for twenty minutes twice a day. He had to be fed via a tube that went down his nose because he hadn't developed his sucking reflex yet, and so the nurses pumped my breast milk down the tube.

Then, just a few days after Eric was born, he started having problems.

His heart started going slower than it was supposed to, and it was then that the doctor realized that my medication was affecting Eric the same way it had been affecting me: by slowing down the heart. He was clearly still "taking" this medication, if you will, via my breast milk. Thus, I continued to pump my milk, but it wasn't given to Eric; instead, I gave it to the doctors for research so they could see how much medicine was in each bottle. And, sure enough, as soon as the medication left Eric's system, he didn't have any more problems.

He was in the NICU for five days in total, after which he was transferred to intermediate for one day and then to growing preemies, where he stayed for five weeks. I went to visit Eric at least three times a day while he was there. Thankfully, the hospital was just about a mile away, so very close by (not that any distance would have kept me away from my son).

A couple of days before Eric came home from the hospital, he had trouble eating. According to the doctors, he wasn't taking his night bottle. I suggested that I stay the night and try to feed it to him myself, but they didn't want me to do this, since I needed my rest, too. "Well, how about you wait until Eric wakes up before giving him the bottle?" I suggested. And, happily, that worked: he took the whole bottle that night. The nurse kept the bottle and put a note on it that said, *Look, Mom, I finished my bottle. Love, Eric.* I still have that bottle in a box of items from Eric's first year. Turned out he hadn't been taking the whole thing before because he'd been more tired than hungry. Mothers' instinct for the win!

He was circumcised before he came home, and when I visited him a few minutes after the procedure, he looked at me as if to say, "You had something to do with that, didn't you?" I felt so bad for him, but I knew it would help him in the long run.

In the end, I took Eric home on April 20, 1990. I was originally supposed to go to my sister's wedding that day, but I couldn't. I love my sister, but getting Eric settled in was my priority at that moment.

Once home, Eric barely took up one fourth of the crib, he was so small. He'd just about reached five pounds at this point.

My routine very quickly turned into hours on end of me just staring at him while he was sleeping. He looked so peaceful and angelic. I couldn't believe that he was home and that he was mine. I got to be a mother now–and God, I was so excited for that journey.

For the first six months of his life, Eric slept in a bassinet perched on my dresser, and for the first few days after our return from the hospital, my mother came to stay with me so she could help me out as I navigated my new motherly duties. She taught me how to use cloth diapers (which I loved using, by the way. He had way less diaper rash because of them), and when Eric finally weighed over ten pounds, I had to have home health aides in the house, since I wasn't supposed to lift or carry anything over his weight. These aides were lovely: they helped me with Eric and my housework, and if I wasn't feeling good, they'd look after Eric until Chris got home.

Meanwhile, Eric got big insanely quickly. It literally seemed as though it happened overnight.

On my very first Mother's Day, Chris, Eric and I went to visit Chris' grandmother, and, of course, we packed Eric's diaper bag with new diapers, formula... everything a baby could need. I told Chris to grab the bag on his way out as I headed out to put Eric in his car seat and get him settled.

We had dinner at Chris' grandmother's while Eric had a nap, and when he woke up, I asked for the diaper bag.

Chris went out to the car... and came back empty handed.

"Where's the bag?" I asked.

"Still on the counter at home. I forgot to grab it," he said sheepishly.

So, I had no food, formula, or diapers for Eric. I felt so bad; like a terrible mother.

Thankfully, Chris' grandmother gave Chris some money so he could go get some diapers and formula and a bottle, and when he left, she told me not to worry; that all new mothers forget something at least once a trip. This made me feel much better. "I did something similar when I had Kathie," she added.

Nevertheless, I learned from that mistake, and made sure I had the diaper bag every time we went out from then on.

When he was about three months old, Eric started sleeping through the night. I remember the first time he did it vividly: it was during the weekend. I woke up and thanked Chris for getting up with the baby during the night, and he said he hadn't.

"I didn't, either," I said, confused.

We both rushed to the bassinet... to find Eric on his back, cooing to himself and waving his hands and feet around.

I was so relieved to see him moving. In that split second, I'd started fearing the worst. I'm a social worker, after all, and had dealt with sudden infant death syndrome a few times. Instead, it turned out Eric was just already super-independent and advanced—which was to become a running theme throughout his childhood!

The doctors had told me that Eric would be delayed because he had been born two months before his due date, and so they set up early interventions for him accordingly, but I knew, intuitively, that he wouldn't be delayed and that he would surpass their expectations. Even still, as planned, I took him to his first assessment, where they said that he was only slightly behind a three-month-old baby who'd been born at full-term. Directly after that appointment, I was on the floor playing with Eric, helping him turn over and sit up. The thing he loved most was when I put a tub of water in front of him and let him splash all he wanted. No concerns here!

His next appointment at early intervention was his last one for motor skills, and they discovered that Eric's left inner ear was slow in developing. They accordingly decided they wanted to keep an eye on this, but this was the full extent of all the concerns they had.

Shortly after this, Chris, Eric and I moved to Springfield, MA, so a) we could be closer to my family and b) Chris could do a co-op program for his degree. This move turned out to be a *huge* blessing, since a couple months after his first birthday, Eric got sick, and I was so grateful I had my mother and sister close by to help me during this time.

I first noticed something was wrong when my sister and I were having a yard sale at my house. On this day, I noticed Eric was very warm upon waking from his nap. I took his temperature, and it was 103.2, so I took him to the emergency room with my mother. By the time we got there, his temperature had soared to one hundred and four. I couldn't even hold him; he was so warm. I put him on the bed and took off some of his clothes to cool him, my hands trembling with worry.

The doctors came in to look at him and quickly discovered he had an ear infection. He was given Tylenol to reduce the fever and antibiotics, and, thankfully, by the time I got him home, he was noticeably cooler.

To this day, I'm very glad my family was there with me during this ordeal: Chris was at work, and so I'd have had to deal with my panic and fear alone. Unfortunately, however, that was the first of many ear infection-induced trips to the ER: Eric had regular ear infections from then until he was about two and a half years old.

It was also around this time (when Eric was two) that I had a hysterectomy due to endometriosis. I had endometriosis all over, including on the sciatic nerve, and so the doctors told me that they could simply scrape it, but it would only come back. Because they didn't want to risk infection, they felt it best to take everything out—and so I signed permission for them to do just that. This was a wise decision: I now have no more back pain, and I don't have to go through a menstrual cycle every month. And, of course, I don't have to worry about getting pregnant again. I've had no problems with my sciatic nerve since then, and my migraines also reduced dramatically.

Besides these things, this time as a family passed pretty peacefully, and it quickly came to our attention that the date we'd always planned to move back to Worcester after Chris finished his co-op was upon us. Chris was still excited to do this, yet when this time rolled around, I felt nothing but concern when I thought about what our housing situation would look like if we followed through with this plan. I didn't exactly want us arriving in Worcester with nowhere to stay now we had Eric. Chris' mother saved the day with this, however, offering to have me and Eric move in with them in Plattsburg, NY. So, I lived with Chris' parents (and Eric, of course) for nine months, Chris visiting us almost every weekend.

Eric and I were staying in the basement, which was very nice: there was wall-to-wall carpeting all throughout the house, so it was very comfortable for us to be staying in. This aside, though, this period (not to mention the ER trips) was a little difficult in and of itself. Specifically, it was difficult to live with my father-in-law, Gopa. I'd lived with Kathie (Chris' mother) before, as we know, and we did fine, but this time was different: I felt like I was constantly treated like a child, and definitely not like an adult who had a child of her own. Gopa and I had always struggled to see eye to eye with one another, and this was only emphasized when we started living together. He is from India, and in his culture, women are supposed to serve men, yet I made it clear from the get-go that I'd never serve him (nor any man, for that matter)—and so he'd respond by telling me I wouldn't be a good Indian wife. I told him I was already married and would serve no man. To me, relationships should be about equality, not servitude.

To illustrate: when I'd been living with Chris' parents for about three months, Amy, Chris' sister (who lived there, too), asked me if I wanted to go to an amusement park in Canada (we lived only thirty minutes away).

"I can't. I have Eric," I said.

Overhearing this conversation, Kathie offered to babysit so I could go—so I thanked her, and Amy and I made our plans.

A few days before we were due to go, Amy and I were discussing the details of our plans during dinner when Gopa asked what I was going to do with Eric. I responded that Kathie would be watching him for me, to which he said, "You wanted the baby, so you should stay home with it." Kathie then explained *she'd* offered to watch Eric for me, and he was quiet after that, but this still left me a little disgruntled. Nobody likes having their parenting questioned, and I was no exception.

Really, though, I didn't have any complaints other than these odd occasions when Gopa would make his (unfavorable) opinion known, so I ultimately counted myself lucky to be under their roof.

Eric meanwhile continued to contract ear infections, so his pediatrician referred him to an ear specialist, who recommended that Eric have tubes put in his ears to prevent these infections. I agreed, and so the surgery was scheduled.

While he was having his surgery, Mom (who had travelled to us so she could support me) and I were sitting, waiting for Eric to get out of the operating room, while I practically trembled with nerves.

"How did you do it when I was small? Having me go through open-heart surgery?" I asked her at one point. I was going crazy with worry, and Eric was only having a minor procedure.

"I didn't have a choice," she said simply. "You were having the surgery so we could make you better, just like Eric is." She paused for a moment, and then continued, "You'll always worry about your children, even when they're adults. It's part of being a mother."

When I was finally buzzed to go back upstairs, I leapt from my seat and was already at the elevator before Mom had even risen from her seat. I was very anxious (as an understatement!) to see Eric again.

When I went to the room, I found Eric crying and fighting with the nurse, trying to take out his IV and pulse ox (sort of like a Band Aid around a finger to measure how much oxygen is in the blood). Once the nurse took the pulse ox off, he calmed down, to my great relief: I hated seeing him in so much distress. I held onto him, and he quieted down a bit, and by the time it was time to take him home, he'd calmed down a lot, and, mercifully, wasn't in so much pain.

That was the first of four times he'd have to undergo that procedure, and I was (thankfully) becoming very relaxed with each one.

A few weeks later, Eric appeared to have diaper rash. I used Desitin, yet this only worsened it. Concerned, I took Eric to the doctor, who told me it was actually a yeast infection, the natural result of all the antibiotics he'd had for his ear infections. She gave me an ointment to put on it... and yet it turned out Eric had an allergic reaction to the ointment: the rash got worse, and every time he wet his diaper, he screamed. I changed him often to relieve him of the discomfort, and, once I took him back to the doctor, she gave me another medicine. Thankfully, that one worked. In a matter of days, his rash looked one hundred percent better, and he was feeling better, too.

Minor health issues aside, Eric was like a ray of sunshine, and was always making his own mischief, much like how I did during my toddler years. Exhibit A: when Eric was still about two years old, Kathie was downstairs in the basement while me and Eric were stood at the top of the stairs. He looked at me and asked if he could go down with Kanga (Eric's attempt at the word "Grandma"), and I said yes. He took the first step successfully... and then tumbled down the rest. Kathie and I froze—and then Eric got up, looked up at Kathie, and said, "Kanga, I tumbled down the stairs, and it was fun! Can I do it again?"

Kathie and I laughed so hard. Eric, bless him, didn't understand why. His tone had been so serious!

Basically, Eric was always getting into (harmless) trouble when he was a boy. Another time (also when he was two), I was writing a five-page paper for one of my classes freestyle on an old computer that I didn't have a hard drive for (you can see where this one is going!) when Eric awoke from his nap, came over to the computer, asked, "What does this do?" and pushed the escape key, erasing my whole paper in the process.

I sat, dumbfounded, and then said, "It puts you upstairs with Kanga."

I took him upstairs to Kathie and told her what he did, who laughed and said, "Eric, stay with Kanga so you live the day to see your third birthday."

The running theme here was that his moments of cheekiness were totally unintentional. As another example, Kathie and I were taking courses at the local college, and most of my courses took place in the evening, when Eric was in bed. One day, Kathie and I were studying for finals while Eric sat on the floor in his room holding a book upside down.

"Eric, what are you doing?" I asked at one point.

"*Shhh*!" he said seriously. "I am studying for finals!"

I bent down, smiled, gave him a hug and kiss, and wished him luck.

Basically, Eric was my pride and joy during this period, and I knew, with vivid clarity, that I was always destined to be his mother.

Eric and I moved out of Chris' parents' house in February 1993, just a month shy of Eric's third birthday (we were moving back in with Chris), and the weekend before, I went up to Chris' to help him pack. It was as I was helping that I found a pile of local newspapers... and noticed that all of them were dog-eared on the personal pages, and that lots of women's ads had been circled. I asked him about this, to which he responded that he was lonely and "looking for a friend".

"You go to college," I reminded him. "You can make friends there, not through personal ads."

"Well, I haven't met anyone."

I only half believed him, but the show must go on.

Despite this small unfortunate revelation, Chris, Eric and I moved into our apartment in the middle of February, and it felt like a huge weight had been lifted now we were all together again. Yet those papers lingered over me like a bad omen, so I tried to talk to him about it, but he wasn't open to discussing.

And it wasn't only in our family life that things were to prove a little tumultuous; my health was also about to take a turn for the worse. Getting pregnant and having Eric had, of course, been a big risk, and so it was somewhat unsurprising when I began having trouble getting my medicine regulated again and getting my irregular heartbeat to calm. At this point, a few years post-partum, I was starting to feel better and certainly had more energy, but my heart never returned to its pre-pregnancy size.

And things were about to get far more interesting in the health department.

When Eric was three, he, Chris and I went to the park to fly Eric's new kite. We all ran around, laughing and having a good time, and after we left the park, Chris and Eric went to grab something in the grocery store while I went into the neighboring department store.

It was then that I started feeling a little funny. I was getting warm, and my vision didn't seem right; it almost seemed tunnel visioned.

I shrugged off my jacket, reasoning that would help, yet I was only getting warmer, and was rapidly feeling worse.

By the time I got to the department I wanted, I couldn't focus, so I decided to leave the store and go find Chris and Eric. It was while I was trying to do this that I ran into a guy and found I couldn't say the words "excuse me"; I was saying them in my mind, but my mouth and voice just couldn't form the words. Meanwhile, my tunnel vision was getting worse, and all I could think of was, *I must get outside and go to the car.* I stumbled out of the store and leaned against a telephone booth. I could see Chris and Eric were in the car already, so I said, "Chris," in what was almost a whisper. Thankfully, Chris looked up, saw me leaning against the telephone booth (probably looking very worse for wear!), and came running to my side. When he got there, I collapsed in his arms.

He carried me to the car and sped off to the hospital. Eric was meanwhile in the back seat, calling, "Mommy! Mommy!" Yet, heartbreakingly, I couldn't answer him.

Fortunately, the hospital was less than a half mile away, though there were a couple of signal lights. This didn't stop Chris, however: for the first time in his life, he ran through two red lights. He honked his horn at anyone in his way and got me to the hospital in less than five minutes.

They took me in right away, and I was told that I'd had a mild stroke.

Specifically, an embolic stroke.

I had a CAT scan done, which showed where the stroke had happened, and (surprise, surprise!) I had to stay in hospital to start another round of medication so they could prevent another one.

Eric overheard the fact that I had to stay in the hospital and was sad. He clambered on a stool so he could see me in bed and told me while the doctor was standing there, "Mommy, if you take your medicine like the doctor tells you, you can come home with Daddy and me."

The doctor smiled sadly. "I want to send you home," he said to me, "but I can't."

I tried to explain to Eric that this was new medicine and that I had to be in hospital so that if it didn't work, they could give me another kind.

"I'll miss you," he said quietly.

"I'll miss you, too."

"You can come to see your mommy any time you want," the doctor said kindly.

And, with that, Eric and Chris went home to eat and change clothes, though they returned later that day to visit me.

I couldn't believe how quickly things can change: I'd been fine running around and having fun one minute, and the next, I was having a stroke. Thankfully, there wasn't much damage from the stroke itself, but I did still have noticeable weakness on my right side, and to this day, I am still a little weaker there. This isn't anything that greatly impacts my quality of life, though.

In the end, I was in the hospital for a total of ten days. It was tough being there knowing that Eric was at home and wanted me there with him, and most of my stay there was just a physical battle of trying to get better and a mental battle of trying not to crumble at the thought of Eric pining after me at home.

A couple of days before I left, the doctors wanted to change one of my regular medicines and give me a loading dose.

"My cardiologist has agreed on that medication, but don't give me a loading dose," I told them quickly. (A loading dose is where they administer more of the medicine to get it at a therapeutic level quickly so that they can then bring the dose down.) "I'm sensitive to medication, and it'd only cause me trouble."

To my dismay, however, they wouldn't listen, and proceeded to give me the loading dose. And, predictably, I had been at home from the hospital for only four days before I started having a terrible reaction to my medicine. I couldn't even sit up without my heart beating very quickly, and I lost my appetite completely.

I called my doctor and told him what I was experiencing, and he told me to come right in. So, yet again, Chris drove me to the hospital, this time with me laying in the backseat so I didn't feel too bad during the drive and Chris pushing me in a wheelchair while we navigated the corridors. It was as Chris was pushing me that everything went black... and the next thing I remember is Chris and the nurses leaning over me, Chris tapping my face and telling me to wake up.

Turns out I had passed out in the chair.

My first words were, "Where's Eric?" to which Chris responded he was with Roseanne, the receptionist. I then asked what had happened, and the nurse said that I'd scared them all; that they thought I was coding on them. (Coding is when someone's heart stops.) My doctor then came into the room and knew exactly what was going on with me after examining me: I was becoming toxic due to the new medicine.

"The doctors from the other hospital gave me a loading dose, and I told them not to," I told him grimly.

"Then you need to be admitted and taken off that medication for a couple of days. Then, you can start on a new medicine."

And so commenced another ten-day hospital stay. More time with Eric I had been cheated out of.

I had a checkup with Dr. Haffajee a few weeks later, which I took Eric with me to. Chris and I had previously explained to Eric that my pacemaker was a battery that helped my heart beat correctly, so as we sat in the waiting room, Eric pointed to an older gentleman sat across from us and asked, "Does he run on batteries, too?"

Wishing the floor would swallow me up, I explained to the gentleman that I had a pacemaker which, to Eric, was a battery that helped my heart beat. The gentleman smiled and answered, "No, son, I do not run on batteries like Mommy."

I smiled, thanked him, and apologized.

"Don't worry," he grinned. "Kids will be kids."

When Eric turned three, I put him in daycare and returned to school. I'd decided pretty much as soon as Eric was born that that was what I was going to do: I'd spend the first three years of his life with him, and then I'd put him in daycare so a) he could be with kids his age and b) I could get my master's degree in social work. And, keeping to my plan, I searched for an adequate daycare a few months before his birthday.

I enrolled Eric one week before I started school, so he had some time to adjust, though it turned out he had no problem with this; it was me who struggled with this adjustment period! I felt empty without him and like I was constantly forgetting something. I cried the first day he went to daycare, and cried on his first day of school, and now, I cry because I can't believe how fast he's growing up and because I wish he were still a baby!

It also turned out I didn't have to take classes for my first semester of school, since I'd been accepted with advance standing credits from my degree in social work. So, instead, I started my internship at an adoption agency close to home while Eric got settled into his new daycare. I was a special needs adoption social worker, trying to find forever homes for children who were over the age of three and had been abused, were from a different culture, and/or were part of a sibling group that the Department of Social Services didn't want to separate. The office was close to home, but I traveled all over the state in my role. This included assessing potential foster and adoptive parents (I visited the family three times before placing a child with them), and then, after a child was placed with them, I'd visit them once a month for six months, until the adoption was finalized.

I enjoyed the work a lot: I got to meet a lot of loving people that were willing to take and love a child that wasn't their own. Of course, there were tough cases, too, though I enjoyed these more than the easy ones. One time, I had a child who was severely developmentally challenged, autistic, and hard of hearing, and had very poor vision and did not like to be restrained. A foster family had this child for about three months before they decided they couldn't adopt him because he was more work than they'd expected and was "taking away from their biological children". It was me who found another home for the child, who later turned into his adoptive family. Tough but rewarding stuff!

I did that internship for the first year of my master's program, of which the second semester was a bit of a challenge, since I had school every Tuesday and Wednesday and my internship every Monday, Thursday, and Friday. I also had studying and a three-year-old child to take care of... *and* a husband. Nevertheless, I got through that semester with good grades—miraculously, I know!

My third semester in the master's program was also rather difficult. During this time, I started my internship at a local hospital—specifically, in the prenatal diabetic clinic, where many of the patients had gestational diabetes. During this placement, I got to see a lot of different things, not least girls having their first baby at thirteen and their second at fifteen. Kids having kids! I felt bad for these girls and made it my mission to help them and make their stay or visit as pleasant as possible. Then, there were the women who were pregnant but who were battling health issues, and these, of course, I could relate to: they wanted the baby and followed the doctors' instructions to a T, but still endured a difficult pregnancy.

Now, of course, not *all* the patients were completely compliant with the doctors' orders; there were several who didn't listen and didn't even seek the proper prenatal care. In those cases, I felt bad for the baby.

Notably, my supervisor at the time became my mentor as the year went on. Margot was a particularly good social worker and knew her stuff about this population.

It was when I was about halfway through this semester that I started having more trouble with keeping my heartbeat regular, though all in all, I'd been doing okay in the health department for a while. That said, for context, "okay" in my book includes having to regularly have my medicine adjusted and/or being put on another medicine frequently, being in and out of hospital for short spells, and having several cardiac ablations (when the doctor threads a catheter through a vein or artery to your heart in your groin and uses lasers to burn out the area that's making the heart fall out of rhythm). They were doing this so often that after no time, I was almost able to do it myself if I wasn't sedated!

The first time I had a cardiac ablation, I remember my back hurting after the procedure and informing the nurses of this. They reported this to the doctors, and then they put a catheter in so I could urinate—and when they did, blood rushed out instead of urine. From there, my blood pressure dropped quickly, and they rushed me to the Cardiac Care Unit to be watched closely. In the end, I had to have blood transfusions and platelets. I refused this at first, considering the AIDS epidemic (I was afraid of contracting it), and, hearing of my concerns, my doctor came in to take care of me at around midnight. Upon entering, he said, "Let's make a compromise. Let us give you platelets, and if that stops the bleeding, we won't give you a transfusion. But if you *don't* stop bleeding within thirty minutes of the platelets starting, we have to give you a transfusion."

I agreed to that.

My doctor then called Chris and my mother to inform them of the plan, the latter arriving at 8AM the following morning to be with me.

Ultimately, I almost had to go in for emergency surgery to stop the bleeding from the platelets, but soon enough, it stopped. I stayed in the ICU for a day, until they knew I was stable.

And Chris? He came in after he'd finished work the next day. He hadn't even called to see how I was doing.

10
HONEY, THERE'S SNOW IN THE ATTIC!

After that procedure, I couldn't go back to work or school until the following semester. And, to top things off, as soon as I got home, Eric came down with chicken pox. He had them all over, but he thankfully wasn't sick with them; he had the same amount of energy he always had. I should have been happy about this, but in a way (though not seriously), I selfishly wished he'd feel a *little* unwell so he would lie down and rest and therefore allow *me* to rest. But he got better before I did and was back in school in no time.

I got back to work three weeks after I was discharged from the hospital, which I very much appreciated, and during that period, in the summer of 1994, I was lucky enough to take advantage of a trip to Ireland the school was sponsoring. We were going to study their social service system, and the trip was great: I saw Dublin, Belfast, and Londonderry, my favorite being Dublin. We visited a college there and sat in on a class, which I enjoyed very much. We also visited an adoption agency, and I was offered a job there that I was very tempted to take, had it not been for my family and friends back in the U.S.

I learned a lot from that trip to Ireland. Over there, they are way more relaxed, and they don't prioritize the almighty dollar (or, more fittingly, the euro). Family is important over there, and families spend lots of time together. And yes, I did get a chance to visit my friend Margaret from high school during my stay!

I started school again after the Christmas break, which was definitely a hard knock back to reality: I had to catch up on the work from the previous semester *while* doing the work from this current semester, so I was very busy. I guess you could say it was reminiscent of my elementary school days, when I'd have to catch up on all my schoolwork on my breaks and at home while sitting in on up-to-date classes! For this period, I went to school, took care of Eric, worked a part-time job, went to my internship, and took care of my husband and a house, all at once. By the end of the semester, I was forced to work fewer and fewer hours because I had too many papers and projects to complete. I also didn't see my family much during this time; I was always either working or doing schoolwork.

And, in among all of this craziness, Chris and I had started to look for a place to buy.

Soon enough, we found a brand-new build in Shrewsbury, MA... but I didn't want to buy just yet, since the company Chris worked for was in the process of being sold, meaning we didn't know if he'd still have a job afterwards.

"Can we still put a bid in?" he asked. "If they don't take it, we'll stop the process."

I agreed to this, knowing they wouldn't take the bid because it was so low. And, sure enough, we didn't get that house, though he did keep his job. I was still glad I'd stuck to my guns with this, however; I was trying to be cautious. I didn't want to get a house only for Chris to lose his job and then us have to move out soon after. So, off we went house hunting again.

During this process, we had to sign a year's lease for the apartment, which was something Chris was very upset about, since it kept us rooted for another year. In fact, he really seemed to be stewing on some resentment: whenever anyone mentioned buying a house, he'd say, " *We* could have been in a house by now, if Karen hadn't talked me out of it," and whenever he was upset with me, he'd say, "Why did I listen to you? We could be in a house right now!"

In the end, the house we found was a mere two houses away from the other one he'd wanted to buy, and was basically exactly the same, with the exception of the color (which I liked better). So, I found someone to take over the lease for the apartment, and we closed on the house on January 27, 1995.

Despite the fact that we'd ultimately both got what we'd wanted, there was a lot of tension between me and Chris during this time. He was still upset over the fact we hadn't got the first house, as well as the fact that we now had to find someone to take over our lease.

It was also around this time that I discovered he was carrying condoms in his jacket pocket. Upon being confronted, he told me that he didn't know why they were there, yet, unfortunately for him, I also found out he'd been downloading pornographic photos from the web. We tried to talk about it, and he promised he wouldn't do it again... and I wanted to believe him.

To add to this, moving in and of itself was stressful. I truly believe now that if a couple can get through buying and moving into a house together, they have a very strong relationship that shouldn't be underestimated!

Throughout this process, I just... didn't know how to feel about me and Chris. I wanted to keep the marriage going for as long as possible. I'd vowed "until death do us part", after all. But that was getting more and more difficult as time went on.

The only thing that helped me during this frenzied period was caring for Eric.

Finally, we moved into our house on January 28, 1995, with the hope that things would be better between us now that we had a place of our own, and, fortunately, I have some happy memories of adventures and contentment in that house. Three weeks after we moved, we had a Nor'easter storm (which is where the snow is coming down hard), during which time I discovered three inches of snow at each end of our attic.

Yes, *in* the attic.

I hurried downstairs and called to Chris, "Umm, honey, is there supposed be snow in the attic?"

"No..."

"Well, there is. About three inches near each window!"

Eric, overhearing this conversation, excitably ran up, ran back down, and said, "Dad, there *is* snow in the attic!"

Chris, frowning, went upstairs to inspect... and then he came back down for a barrel and shovel. As I watched him shovel the snow into the barrel, faintly amused,

I said, "Why don't you open the window and throw the snow out of it?"

"I don't want to get it on Brian's lawn."

"Well, I'll bet Brian already *has* snow, and just a little bit more won't hurt."

So, Chris shoveled the snow out of the attic. It looked like something out of a sitcom!

After that, we had the builders come out and fix the roof so no more snow or rain could come in, and then, in the spring, I opened the window over the sink... and it fell off the hinges and fell in the backyard! Eric wasted no time in dashing upstairs and telling Chris, "Mommy broke the kitchen window!"

Thanks, kid.

Chris immediately came downstairs to find the window missing and me sheepishly stood before what was now a massive hole in the wall.

Throw into the mix the fact that all of this was happening in a brand-new house, and the situation becomes either insanely stressful or insanely comical—I'll let you decide which! We talked to other house owners on our street about this, and it turned out they had similar complaints, so make what you will of that.

Still, in among all this craziness, there were certainly pockets of peace (and humor!) to be found in our new day-to-day life. A few months after we moved in, Eric and I naturally fell into a routine every day after we got home (he was five at the time): we'd come in and I'd go through the mail while Eric helped himself to a drink. This was a sweet little routine, and one that I quickly grew to treasure. One time, when we were doing this, Eric asked if he could get himself a drink, and he proceeded to jump on the counter to get one of his glasses (they were the Tupperware glasses), and, as he was jumping off, the leg of his shorts got caught on the knob of the cabinet below the counter. This meant that for a good few seconds, Eric was hanging upside down, shouting, "Mom, can you help me?"

When I turned around and saw him hanging upside down, I couldn't help but laugh. He wasn't hurt, mind; just hanging upside down with this shocked expression on his face.

Eric sighed and said, "When you're done laughing, can you get me down?"

Rest assured, I pulled him off the cabinet and got him his drink.

I immediately called Kathie to tell her what had happened, which took me a while, since I physically couldn't stop laughing. Once I (finally) got the story out, she was laughing, too. "It wasn't *that* funny," Eric meanwhile huffed in the background.

Of course, I also told Chris the story when he got home, but he didn't think it was funny. But this didn't deter me in remaining thoroughly amused: to this day, when I think of it and see Eric hanging upside down from the cabinet, I laugh hysterically.

There was another time that Eric and I were making pie dough. After we finished the pies and as we were cleaning up, a flour fight broke out. It started with me putting a dab of flour on Eric's nose. He returned the favor... and then we were patting flour on each other's faces, and it took off from there! Chris walked in the middle of this, and Eric immediately said, "She started it!"

I smiled, put my floury hands on his head, and said, "But he *continued* it!"

Eric was covered in flour from head to toe. Chris offered to help clean the mess–and it was a *big* mess–and when I brushed this off, he asked how else he could help.

"Well, you can choose, since Eric and I made the mess," I laughed. "You can clean up the kitchen or give Eric a bath or shower."

He went for the latter option... and he failed to consider the key detail that water and flour make a paste. This meant it took him twice as long to clean Eric as it did me to clean the kitchen.

These moments of fun were abundant, but with every up inevitably comes a down.

Slightly later in 1995, I had another stroke due to my irregular heartbeat. I was coming home from work one day when I realized I felt odd: I was having tunnel vision, and my right side was tingling. I focused on getting home and then called Chris at work, who told me to call the doctor. So, I did, and he immediately instructed me to go to the ER. Chris insisted that he couldn't leave work, so I drove myself to the hospital. The doctors ran some tests, determined it was a painless headache, and discharged me. Yet I still felt weak on my right side the next day, so I called my doctor and told him what was going on, to which he responded that he wanted to see me in his office the next day. I went to this appointment still feeling weak on my right side, and he said that, sure enough, I'd had another small stroke. I told him about my weakness from the previous stroke, and he prescribed physical therapy so I could regain my strength. In the meantime, he put me on another medication to prevent another stroke from happening.

In the end, I was in physical therapy for three months, and it worked wonders: I emerged with around the same level of strength that I'd had before the stroke—and I've not had another to date! This was thanks to the aspirin and warfarin (a blood thinner) I was on for the following two decades. Thank God for medicine!

May 6, 1995, was mine and Chris' anniversary, as well as the last day of school, so I worked hard to finish all my work and received my reports from every teacher for the present and all past semesters on May 5—and, to my surprise, I didn't get below a B-plus for any of the work I passed in.

I was thrilled!

I graduated with the rest of my class with pride. I still had a few hours of my internship to finish, but that was easy compared to what I had been doing. I was also offered a job at the hospital after my graduation, and this was all because my supervisor believed in me. She was technically taking a risk on me, considering my heart problems, but she knew I could do the work, and so she took the chance.

I hope I can give someone else such an amazing opportunity in the future.

While I was glad to have some of the pressure off my daily routine and commitments, after everything calmed down, all was said and done, and the only thing on my agenda was now completing my shifts at the hospital, I felt a little aimless: I'd been doing so much for so long that I'd started to get used to it, and now that I'd finished everything, I realized that all was left for me was... work. Bog-standard shift work.

I learned to fill my spare time with my family, however, which filled me with much happiness. And the fact still stood that I had been determined to get my master's... and I had. As I've mentioned, my motto is, "They told me I couldn't. That is why I did," and I think that shows here! Hence, I was *extremely* excited when I finally got my master's degree because I'd proven *I could do it with* the right support, encouragement, and determination.

When Eric and I had been living with Kathie and Gopa, I'd taken a few courses toward my master's, and one of the professors at SUNY Plattsburgh had told me I would never get the full qualification. Well, that didn't stop me! It may have taken me a couple of years and a few trips to the hospital, but I now had my master's, and I felt on top of the world for it. Plus, getting my master's degree opened up more job opportunities for me. I changed jobs a few times before I landed my dream job, which is what I am still doing today: working with transplant patients in a hospital.

All was aligned, and I had nothing but my own determination and ruthlessness to thank. And *that* was something to be proud of.

About a year after I started working at the hospital, I had an incident with my heart. I was in my office talking to my intern one day when it started going really fast and falling out of rhythm. Taking a mental note of my symptoms and concluding that something must be wrong, I calmly rose, went to my manager's office, and said, "Joanne, my heart is out of rhythm and going fast. Do I go down to the ER, or to employee health?"

Joanne glanced up and eyed me with concern. "I'll walk you to the ER."

I asked the receptionist on duty to inform my intern that she could go home and that I'd see her on Monday.

Joanne and I were climbing down the stairs to the ER (the elevator was too slow) when she turned to me and said, "Once we get to the ER, you're going to sit down, and I'll get a nurse to help you."

"Okay."

I used to work in this ER, so all the doctors and nurses knew me already. This meant there was some hubbub when I walked in. "What's going on?" one nurse asked me.

"The usual. My heart is out of rhythm and it's going about one hundred and twenty to one hundred and fifty beats per minute."

She sprang into action: she put me in a room and on the monitor, and, indeed, my heart was going at exactly one hundred and twenty beats per minute. The team called my doctor in Boston and wanted me to stay the night so I could be transported to Boston the following morning.

I called Chris to let him know I was being admitted to hospital... again.

And the chaos didn't stop there.

In September 1996, a mere eighteen months after our move to our new house,

Chris (as predicted and feared by me) was laid off from his job, which inevitably led to us having money problems. I was still working full-time, and he was under the strain of looking for a job, so he and I were very stressed over our schedules and whether we could make the bills. This sadly resulted in us arguing a lot.

Then, to add insult to injury, at the end of September, I found out that Chris had signed up to an online dating service. He'd responded to a few ads and was ready to meet this woman. I still don't know whether he actually did or not. He said he didn't, but to be quite honest, I didn't believe him.

I asked him to move out of the house, which he didn't do quickly—and in the interim, we started seeing a marriage counselor. Yet things never seemed to be resolved, and he never wanted to admit that some of the problems we faced in our marriage were his fault.

In the end, Chris moved out for a few months, and I thought this period would allow us to straighten things out.

Nope.

He moved back in in February 1997, and by March, we were fighting again: he was answering personal ads from the paper and calling 1-900 numbers. (He denied this, but I had the phone bills to prove it.) So, I went away with my mother to Nashville, TN, for ten days, and in that time, I made the conscious decision to try to make this marriage work. Yet when I got home, things were no different: he was still calling these women and going out on Friday nights until 2AM.

I finally told him he would have to sleep in the guestroom while I took the master bedroom.

We lived like that for about nine months. In every way that mattered, we were living as roommates instead of husband and wife.

I remember one day during this period, I had just arrived home with groceries, and, as I was unloading them from the car, he came over and said he was hungry.

"Well, if you help me with the groceries, you'll get to have dinner faster," I responded—so he took two bags in and then went to watch TV, leaving me to grab the rest and put everything away. He came back in a few moments later, again complaining from hunger and asking when supper was going to be ready.

"I started while I was putting away the groceries," I said shortly, Eric meanwhile balanced on my hip. Chris was clearly oblivious to how ludicrous this image was: me wrestling groceries, a toddler, and dinner while he sat in front of a TV screen complaining of hunger.

I heard Chris mumble something before walking away, so I shouted after him, "Sure, walk away instead of talking about it!"

He wheeled around and said, "Do you want me to fucking come over there and hit you instead?" and turned to leave again.

"Fine! Leave! And while you're out, you can get something to eat!"

After that event, I knew I couldn't stay there much longer, so, on January 1, 1998, Eric and I moved into a little house in Worcester, MA, a few miles away from Chris. I was happier after this change, but was also struggling financially, since Chris refused to pay child support. In the end, however, I rose to the occasion: I paid the rent, put food on the table, and paid all my other bills alone. It was difficult, but I did it. Besides, you can't put a price on peace.

It was also around this time that I was instructed to cut my work hours to twenty per week. Joanne, my manager, had initiated a short-term disability application, and once it went into effect, she didn't want me to come back to work.

Sure enough, the short-term disability was approved, and the hospital had a going-away party for me.

"You're not fired," Joanne made a point of saying to me, "you're going on medical leave. But if you come to work on Monday, I *will* fire you."

Straight after this, I had to move again because the landlord wanted the house back. I was lucky to find an apartment about one mile away from the place I was living in, but this was still a big inconvenience while caring for a young child, as an understatement.

Shortly thereafter, Chris and I started seeing a mediator to help us with the divorce agreement, and we filed for divorce in July 1998 and were officially divorced on September 3, 1998.

I was very happy that day. Pretty much immediately after the divorce was finalized, I could see the old, cheerful Karen coming back. I realized I had been becoming a person I didn't want to be, and now, here I stood, a single parent to a wonderful son. I knew that through my strength, I was showing him that people could survive anything if they kept fighting.

I must admit that it initially felt weird being divorced, yet I knew I was doing the right thing and that even if I'd tried harder, the marriage just wouldn't have worked. The bottom line was, I wasn't happy in my marriage, and it wasn't good for Eric to grow up in a place where no one was happy. Chris and I being divorced, while not technically ideal, meant Eric got to have quality alone time with both his mom and his dad—though he, too, took a while to adjust. It was difficult for him, but I was there for him whenever he needed me. And the fact we only lived four miles away from Chris certainly helped and meant Eric could see his father whenever he wanted.

In the end, we organized for Chris to see Eric on Wednesdays and every other weekend, though he always had the option to see Eric if he called and suggested other times. I didn't want to keep Eric from his father; yes, I was divorcing Chris, but that didn't have to affect Eric's relationship with him.

So, yes, this adjustment was difficult and often confusing. I was happy and sad at the same time, and money was tight (I was making half of what Chris was and was being given zero financial support). Plus, I had to deal with my health issues, which obviously never fully went away. But I never gave up, and my focus was on providing for Eric and myself—an attitude that ultimately served me well and that I wouldn't change if I had to go back and do it all again.

In October 1998, I started experiencing shortness of breath, and wasn't feeling well. I went to see my cardiologist in light of this, who performed several tests and informed me that I may need a heart and lung transplant. Apparently, my heart had weakened, and the only thing that would help it was a double transplant.

Wow.

I wanted to get another opinion before signing up for the transplant (obviously it would be a very big decision!), so I went to Brigham and Women's Hospital, who echoed the same thing: I needed a transplant. So, I went for a *third* opinion at Boston Children's Hospital, and my doctor there explained exactly what was happening to my heart. "The valves are like swinging doors, and in your heart, the doors aren't closing all the way, and one of them also has a hole in it."

With that, I called Chris to let him know I was being admitted to hospital from the clinic to do a test and perform a catheterization.

In the end, I was in the hospital for a week, during which time Eric stayed with

Chris. I was then temporarily discharged so I could get some things together in advance of what would be my sixth open-heart surgery. My return home ended up being short-lived, however: a few days later, I was re-admitted because I was having a lot of difficulty breathing, even when just doing basic things around the house. It was as they were running a test that my pacemaker battery started to run out.

When it rains, it pours.

I was also having palpitations and my heartbeat was irregular, and so the doctors brought my surgery forward so they could also replace my pacemaker.

Right before this (during that post-hospital, pre-surgery period while I was getting stuff ready for Eric so he could stay at his father's while I was at the hospital), Chris told me that during my time in hospital, Eric's teacher had called him to see if he needed her to go to the store to get Eric some clothes. Turned out Chris had been sending Eric to school in the same clothes he'd arrived at Chris' in, as well as one of Chris' sweaters.

"Why didn't you have someone come to my apartment and grab some stuff for Eric?" I demanded, bewildered.

"Oh. I hadn't thought of that."

Dumbfounded, I tried to explain to him that Eric's teacher could have called the Department of Social Services and reported to them that Eric was being neglected.

"Well, she didn't," Chris sighed, "and now Eric will have clean clothes."

After this (rather frustrating) encounter, it was time to explain to Eric that I had to go back to the hospital for heart surgery... and to keep at bay my concern at the thought of him living with Chris for any extended period of time. Chris has clearly proven himself to lack common sense in the parenting department during my previous stay, and so I felt some real trepidation at this plan. Yet I had no other choice, and the night before the surgery, Eric, Chris, and my mom came to see me.

"When are you coming home?" Eric asked.

"I'm going to have surgery, and then when the doctors feel that I'm better, I'll be home."

It was then that the surgeon came in to talk to me and my mom about the surgery.

"Could you wait until Eric goes home?" I asked.

He nodded understandingly, and then Eric asked him, "Will my mommy be, okay?"

"I will make your mommy much better," he nodded. "Mommy may not talk to you for a few days, but when she is able to talk on the phone, she'll call you."

"Okay. Just make sure you make her feel better."

"I will."

After that, Eric and Chris left, and the doctor started explaining how the surgery was going to go and what to expect after it. The following day (as planned), I was prepped for the surgery and then wheeled to the operating room, my mother by my side the whole time, as she always had been.

The next thing I remember is waking up in the Cardiac Care Unit... and being in a lot of pain. I still had the tube down my throat when I woke up. My mom came into the room soon thereafter, however, and this put me at ease. Plus, I had a button for pain medicine, which was helpful, though I tried not to use it too often: I don't like the sleepiness of being on pain medicine, nor do I like the feeling of being drugged up.

Once I got the tube out and was breathing on my own, the first words I said were, "I forgot about the pain."

Just one day after the surgery, however, I was up and walking around the cardiac unit—slowly, mind, but walking, nonetheless. I was on the cardiac unit for about three days before I was transferred to the regular unit, where I stayed for about a week and a half. I was getting stronger every day, and after that week, I was able to go home, though I couldn't drive for six weeks. The good part was that I was still on short-term disability, so I was still getting paid while being out. No need to repeat the nightmare that had ensued last time I'd been unable to work post-hospitalization.

A crazy year indeed. Yet here I was, fighting against the odds!

I had recovered from my sixth open-heart surgery, and I was doing well.

Eric also started at a new school in January of 1999, and so this in itself was a period of adjustment... yet the hardest thing to get used to was still the divorce. And this wasn't because of any nostalgia or regret or struggle; on the contrary, it was largely because Chris was still trying to call all the shots at every opportunity. He often came over unannounced, yet insisted I had to call before I went to *his* house. He also sometimes wouldn't take Eric on his weekend because he'd "made other plans".

Blessedly, a well-timed break away from all of this controlling behavior presented itself that June. Joanne was having her wedding in North Carolina and wanted me to be her Maid of Honor and to watch her girls while she was on her honeymoon. Of course, I accepted. Before that trip, however, I ended up in hospital (again) with another bout of bacterial endocarditis for two weeks. After that, I had a visiting nurse come to my house to assist with my medication.

While I was in NC some weeks later, I kept half an eye open for any good properties that were available. Joanne had wanted me to move down for some time, and I found myself half-seriously pondering this while I was there. And, sure enough, while on this trip, I found the perfect house, and the plan was for my ex-sister-in-law, Caren, to move down with me and Eric with her daughter, Sam.

I signed the papers on the house, and with that, Eric and I moved in on August 1, 1999 (though in the end, Caren didn't move down with me. She decided at the last minute not to come).

One week after I got to NC, I was due for an appointment with my new cardiologist at Duke University Hospital. At that appointment, my cardiologist's colleague looked at my pacemaker, moved his hand around it, and said, "You have an infection on the pacemaker, and you'll be on antibiotics for the rest of your life—which will be a short life if you don't get the pacemaker out and get rid of the infection." He then accordingly scheduled me to come into the hospital on August 25, when he would perform the surgery.

One week later, I became very sick, unable to keep anything down, running a fever, and rapidly losing weight. Joanne had to take me to the ER, where it became clear that the infection was worsening. Looking back now, there are a few days of that hospital stay that I don't remember at all. All I know is that I was very sick: my kidneys were shutting down, and the infection was spreading. However, the team there were able to get the infection under control so they could perform the surgery earlier, during which they would remove my pacemaker and leads. After the surgery, I was given an external pacemaker because they'd let the infection drain and wanted to make sure it was fully gone before they put in another pacemaker.

Now, external pacemakers are usually only used for a short period—and I had mine in for about ten days, while I was experiencing an irregular heartbeat. There was one day where my heart was so out of rhythm that it wouldn't fall back into a normal beating pattern. When I noticed this, I asked the nurse to page the residents so they could take a look, and the nurse obliged—four or five times, at that—yet they didn't answer. I then called the hospital operator and had my cardiologist (the chief of cardiologists) paged, and after I explained what was happening, he told me to page the residents.

"The nurse has paged them four or five times, with no response."

The doctor paused. "I'm at a conference out of state, but I'll page the residents."

Sure enough, within about five minutes, the residents arrived.

"We've been paging you tons, and we didn't receive an answer once," I remarked upon their arrival. They told me they were on the rounds, to which I responded, "I spoke with the chief of cardiology, and he knows you've been ignoring my pages."

"Why did you do that?" one of them said quickly, betraying a hint of panic.

"Because he's my doctor. And you'll all be getting a call from him. He's not pleased with your performance. I'm glad I wasn't coding, or I'd be dead! Not exactly an effective way to start your careers. Now, please leave my room and never come back."

My doctor then called my nurse and gave her orders for another medication to give me, which helped immensely.

Moral of the story: stand up for what you know you need.

In the end, I finally got the new pacemaker, and felt much better. This also meant I was finally able to go home (after six weeks of hospitalization, from August 15 until October 1), though my mother had to accompany and care for me for some time, since I still had some issues: the medication I was taking for the infection was vancomycin and gentamycin, which I was to continue taking for over one hundred days, and this affected my balance. When I sat up, I had triple vision and didn't know which figure was real. So, while my mom was staying with me, she helped me get Eric ready for school and get to my medical appointments.

In total, she stayed for a little over a week, and I felt miles better after this period. I still couldn't drive, but that was okay: Joanne lived six houses away, and she and her girls helped immensely. And after about one month, I was doing even better. I was also going to balance therapy during this period, and every time I asked how I was doing, my therapist said, "There is room for improvement"—and she was right: it was quite easy for me to lose my balance. I remember one time, Eric walked by me in the hall and barely touched me with his shoulder, yet I still lost my balance and fell backwards into the wall. He apologized profusely for this, but he'd of course done nothing wrong. With time, however, my balance improved, and today, I still have balance issues when on uneven terrain, especially if it's dark. If I have to go up or down a curb or some steps, I hold onto a friend's arm or a railing. Nevertheless, my healing was exponential, though I did continue to dip in and out of hospital from the time I was released (October 1999) to April the following year.

The absolute hardest part of this undoubtedly was being away from my family. It was also a pretty intense time for my body: I was in a new place with a new doctor and was rapidly learning how my body healed and reacted to medication.

This period was also hard on Eric for the same reasons... and it was also around this time, when Eric was thirteen, that I found out he was using drugs.

This was initially almost impossible for me to wrap my head around, but the evidence spoke for itself—so, going into autopilot mode, I reported it to the school and gave them permission to search his locker (though they didn't find anything).

Of course, Eric was very mad at me for this, and demanded, "What mother would do that to her son?"

"A mother who wants her son to live!" I shot back.

For all his shock, this experience didn't put him off. He only got into the harder drugs, which led to me having to kick him out of the house. After that, he went to stay with his girlfriend, who was using, too.

As you can very well imagine, this marked the beginning of a very, very trying journey with Eric and his drug use, and, naturally, thoughts, worries, and suspicions about this plagued me during all hours of the day.

At least things on the career front were going swimmingly while it felt as though everything was crumbling around me at home. I got my first job in NC as a social worker at a nursing home, and I enjoyed working alongside most of the people there. I corresponded most with my co-worker, Jill; she and I had a monthly rotation of who oversaw admissions.

At one point, Jill was on vacation for a week, and I set the record for admissions: I had seven new admissions, two re-admits, and I completed all my work *and* hers in one day. It's safe to say the owners were happy with me!

Then, on July 31, 2003, Jill and I had just finished lunch and I was in the office doing my work on my computer when I felt myself falling forward and hitting my head on the desk... and the next thing I knew, I was waking up in a hospital. While I was passed out, I had a bunch of what can only be described as visions: I saw my grandmother, who had passed away three years before, and she told me to "go back to my mother and shut the door". I then saw my friend who lived a few miles away get the call about me, go to her boss' office, and get in her boss' son's car, who then drove her to hospital.

Talk about strange.

When I opened my eyes at the hospital, I saw that same friend and Eric hovering over me.

"What happened?" I asked groggily.

They told me—and then everything went black again.

I do remember asking to be transferred to Duke, which I was, as I found out the next morning when I opened my eyes again.

I dimly registered my keen chest pains and a number of people coming into my room again, and it was after a while of lying there that I realized that the pain was being caused by a two-hundred-and-fifty-pound person doing chest compressions. Then, my doctor came in and explained what had happened: I'd had a cardiac arrest and had been down for two minutes and forty-four seconds. I had been sixteen seconds away from permanent brain damage. And, indeed, I did suffer short-term memory loss for a while: my mom would call, and right after the conversation, I'd forget what had even been said.

My cardiologist decided I urgently needed a defibrillator/pacemaker combo.

While I was in hospital, Jill and the administrator came to visit me. "You could have just asked for the time off," she joked at my bedside.

"Yeah, but when you die at work, you're *guaranteed* time off," I responded.

I ended up staying in hospital for a week, but couldn't go back to work until August 20, around two weeks after I was discharged. Further, after the defibrillator was implanted, my doctor had to report it to the DMV, who instructed me to turn in my driver's license for six months.

"Why?" I queried.

"You've had an unplanned cardiac arrest and now have a defibrillator, so you must be episode free for six months before we can permit you to drive."

"But I need to work. And *no* one plans a cardiac arrest."

"I'm afraid it's the rules, ma'am."

So, I turned in my license and acquired a state ID instead. Thankfully, I was able to hitch a ride from one of my dieticians (who lived nearby) so long as I changed my shifts to accommodate his, which my supervisor agreed to.

Going back to work was a little surreal: the people there hadn't counted on me coming back, which is always a strange atmosphere to walk into. Regardless, I had a "welcome back" sign across my office door the day I returned, which made me feel really special and wanted. One thing that was funny, though, was that the owner of the nursing home seemed to begrudge standing any more than two feet away to me; people said he'd been speaking to me the moment I'd collapsed, so he was a little spooked and thus was avoiding talking to me, lest it should happen again. That lasted a couple of weeks, and then (gladly) things went back to normal. The defibrillator also helped a lot of health-wise: my heartbeat stayed regular, and I didn't need to go into the hospital much, which was very welcoming.

And, of course, I didn't let these health problems stop me from living my life to the fullest.

In 2005, I turned forty-two years old, and to celebrate my birthday, I went skydiving for the first time with my friend, Susan–after my mandatory 6AM call with my mom, of course.

We went through the class and got suited up, and before I knew it, we were on the plane and fifteen thousand feet in the air.

Susan jumped first; I heard her scream, "*Oop*–" before she was abruptly cut off by the distance between us.

And then I was next.

The guy I was doing the skydive with told me to cross my arm in front of me. Then, he said, "Are you ready?"

"I guess s–"

We were out of the plane before I could finish my sentence.

We were *freefalling*.

My heart was pounding a mile a minute, my skin was flapping in the wind, and I felt (quite literally) on top of the world.

The whole thing was also recorded, which was a great idea.

Once we got to six thousand feet, the parachute opened, and we were floating to the ground. The view was *gorgeous*, and it was very serene and quiet up there.

In a nutshell, it was awesome.

When Susan and I got back to my car, I called Mom again. "Hi, Mom!"

Immediately able to decipher the excitement and adrenaline coursing through my voice, my mom wearily said, "What did you do, Karen?"

"I just jumped out of a *plane*!"

She wasn't too happy.

"I'm alright, Mom!"

"Hmm. Okay."

Susan and I went to breakfast after that, though we could barely sit still or keep quiet as we ate high on adrenaline for most of that day.

So, that was how I celebrated my forty-second birthday. And if that isn't the biggest "screw you" to my heart condition, I don't know what is.

11
IT'S TIME FOR A CHANGE

Before my sixth open-heart surgery, there had been (as I have mentioned) some talk about me having a heart transplant, though it wasn't certain at that time whether I needed a heart *and* lung transplant. This remained unsettled.

Three months after my forty-second birthday, I started having problems with my heart once again. It was a couple of weeks before Christmas when I ended up in Duke again: my heart was out of rhythm and getting weaker and weaker, though I tried to view the whole thing in a positive light. I like trying to create my own fun even though I'm not feeling good, and I wasted no time in doing this in the examining room at Duke. Once the nurse came in and began asking me the routine demographic information-related questions, starting with, "What is your name?" I fired back, "Karen. What's yours?"

(I don't remember his response, so let's just say it was) "Greg. What is your date of birth?"

I told him and asked him for his.

"I don't need to answer that one," he said cautiously.

I said, with a smile on my face, "You're asking me all these personal questions so you can treat me. *I* need to know all these answers, so I know *who* is treating me."

He smiled and told me his birthday.

My friend Katie and her mother were in the room with me while this exchange was occurring, and at this moment, I could hear them saying, "Can you believe she's doing this?"

"Greg" and I continued in our little back-and-forth... until my heart decided to spike up to about one hundred and twenty. Then, I was transported to Duke in Durham ("Big Duke"), where I stayed for about ten days. During my stay, the team mentioned I may need a transplant in two to three years. "Okay," I said calmly, trying not to read into this too much. Then, the matter was dropped, and they swiftly signed me up for cardiac rehab.

This was my third time going through rehab, though I didn't start this round until January 2006 due to the holidays. From then on, I went three days a week on every Monday, Wednesday, and Friday.

I was partaking in my third session when I suddenly got really dizzy and my blood pressure dropped. Surprise, surprise, I had to go to the ER of "Small Duke", where I was quickly transferred to "Big Duke" yet again.

It's safe to say this was all getting a little repetitive at this point.

It was then that Dr. Cantor, my cardiologist, came in to see me and informed me that I needed a transplant now.

"Wait a minute, *now*?" I echoed, stupefied. "A few weeks ago, I was told I may need a transplant in two to three years. And now you're saying I need it *now*?"

"Two to three years, two to three weeks, what's the difference?" he joked.

"A *lot*. Years." It was like my pregnancy: I'd unexpectedly had Eric two months early, and now, I was having a *transplant*, of all things, two *years* early. I started to seriously wonder in that moment if doctors had a completely different concept of time to the rest of us.

Dr. Cantor sobered and pressed on, "We're going to start the evaluation process while you're here."

Let me tell you, this was the most intense physical of my *life*. I saw a financial person, a psychologist, and a social worker, and I also had about twenty tubes of blood taken (not exaggerating), *and* I had to see my gynecologist for an exam. I had to have my first ever mammogram and CT scans, and a ream of other such tests. If anything at all came up on any one of the tests, they had to take more.

When I visited the psychologist and social worker (whose role was to evaluate my mental health and how I would cope with the transplant), I told them both that *I* wasn't sick, but that my *heart* was sick, so if they took my sick heart out and gave me a healthy one, I'd remain healthy and live a well-rounded life from then. "I also think I'll be pretty sad for the person whose heart I get, since that person had to die so I could live, but I have to remember that I didn't kill that person. I'll mourn their death, and I'll take care of their heart—the gift of life they gave me."

Suffice to say I passed that assessment with an all-clear.

I was also introduced to the cardiologist that would take over my care after the transplant by Dr. Cantor. "Karen, this is Dr. Rogers; Dr. Rogers, this is Karen."

Dr. Rogers came over to shake my hand before stating, "I don't think you can do this."

Dr. Cantor swiftly interrupted Dr. Rogers with, "Don't tell this woman she can't do anything, because she'll prove you wrong. Her parents were told she wasn't going to live to see her first birthday, and she is now forty-two. She lived through the Mustard procedure. She was told she couldn't get pregnant, and she now has a fifteen-year-old boy at home. This woman knows how she feels and likes a doctor who listens to her."

Dr. Rogers looked at me again and said, "Okay, let's start this again."

And with all that cleared up, Dr. Rogers examined me and informed me of the process behind the transplant.

I went home a couple of days later, continued with my cardiac rehab, and waited to see if I was going to be listed. The call came sooner than expected: February 27, 2006. "Okay, so we have two options," the transplant surgeon said. "We can either repair your valve again, or you can get a transplant."

I paused. "I've had six open-hearts surgeries, and the last one was seven years ago and was supposed to repair the valve. So, if we set out to repair the valve again, I'll be in this same situation seven years from now, only then, I will be seven years older and seven years weaker. I know this transplant isn't a cure, but I *will* have a better quality of life for it."

"I agree, Karen. I'll go to the committee and see what they say."

The very next day, I got a call from Duke informing me that I was going on the transplant list. I took this moment to inform my coordinator that I had a cruise planned for the middle of March, and she said they'd remove me from the list for the week I was gone and then put me back on it when I returned.

Meanwhile, my heart was pumping at about fifteen percent (the normal level is sixty percent and over), but at this point, that was just my normal. After all, I'd never had a normal or healthy heart. But maybe, just maybe, that was about to change.

Practically no time elapsed between my cruise and my surgery. On April 6, 2006 (my dad's birthday), my phone rang at 3:52AM, and when I answered, the voice on the other end of the line asked, "When did you eat last?"

"Um, about ten?"

"What did you eat?"

I looked at the phone, still half-asleep, wondering who was calling me. "Pasta," I answered groggily.

"And what are your allergies?"

I was waking up around this point, and so the penny dropped. "You're Beth!"

She laughed. "Thank you for waking up!"

She proceeded to explain that I was now first in line for a heart donation and that they wanted me at the hospital so they could be ready to operate when it happened. I agreed, and after hanging up, I called Katie, my friend, who we had planned in advance would give me a ride to the hospital.

"Shit!" was all I heard on the other end of the line before she hung up. I then called my mom and told her that Katie may be picking her up from the airport because I'd been called into hospital. (We'd already made plans for her to visit me for a week, so she already had the flight booked.)

After that, I called my friend, Paul. And all the while, in among making these phone calls and trying to process what was happening, I was running around my house trying to wake up Eric to let him know I was going to the hospital. At one point, I forced myself to stop so I could gather my thoughts for a second... and when I looked down, I remembered, *Dang, I have to get dressed.*

Immediately after I was dressed, I called Katie again and asked where she was, to which she said, "I'm pulling in your driveway." And with that, she picked me up, and we were whizzing down the road at 4:15AM, not even half an hour after I'd picked up the phone to Beth.

We got to an intersection where a man was laying in the road. I said, "I guess I'm not getting *his* heart."

Katie, undeterred, made a U-turn and headed the other way. She was evidently nervous and was driving *way* too fast.

"Katie, they won't give me a heart if I arrive there dead," I reminded her.

She took the hint and slowed down, and when we arrived, I was immediately admitted.

The doctors completed a round of tests... and then we waited.

At about 11AM, I was told the heart was too big for me, and so it went to someone else.

Talk about an anticlimax.

I was disappointed, but I understood, and they reassured me that I'd be bumped up on the list since my heart was worsening.

Basically, my trip to hospital was a dry run, as they call it in the medical field. So, I left and went to pick my mom up at the airport.

When she saw me, she said, "I know Duke is good, but having a heart transplant and being out the same day is really quite extraordinary."

I gave her a small smile and explained why I hadn't gotten the heart. She was disappointed, too, but her visit (which was to last a week) helped to take the sting off.

When it was time for her to leave, I felt really quite despondent: I would miss her, and she'd been a huge help with the laundry and meals while I was growing weaker and weaker.

Two weeks after Mom left, I got my second call for a heart. It was April 21, 2006, and I had just dropped Eric off at school and was talking with my friend, Lory. It had been her birthday the day before, and she was returning the call I'd tried to make but she hadn't been able to pick up on the day.

While we were talking, I got a beep signaling a waiting call. Recognizing the number, I quickly said to Lory, "Hold on, please; it's Duke calling."

It was my coordinator, who quickly told me that there was another heart that I was second in line for, and the hospital were still deciding if I needed to be called in. "I'll call back in twenty minutes," she said.

So, I got back on my call with Lory. "They have a heart, but I'm second in line," I told her hurriedly.

"Oh, wow. Okay, I should let you go, then!"

"Yeah. I love you!"

"Love you."

Then Beth called back, who said, "Yeah, they want you in the hospital."

I called Katie and told her that they want me in... and the chaos commenced. On the way to the hospital, I called Eric's school and told them what was going on, but asked them not to tell him right away, since he had midterms that day. They promised they would tell him before the last bell.

It was rush hour, so it took a little longer than last time to get to the hospital, but, soon enough, I was admitted, placed in a room, and told to shower. That was my second shower in two hours—only for this shower, they gave me these scrubbing sponges that had soap in them. Katie handed me one and then the other one as I scrubbed at my chest with them, and by the time I emerged, my chest was so clean that it was bright red from all rigorous scrubbing. Soon thereafter, Katie's mother arrived, and we waited. This was at about 9AM. We were also soon joined by my pastor friend, who had come to visit me.

I got a call from my coordinator at around 12PM, and she told me if the heart was mine, I'd know at around 3PM. I quickly called my mother and mother-in-law to let them know what was happening.

Soon enough, 3:10PM rolled around, and I got the call that the heart was mine and that they'd come in to get me soon. And they sure did! Suddenly, several people came into my room, all asking for my name and date of birth. "We're taking you to the operating room," they said swiftly, and while they resumed their buzzing around, I got back on the phone to Kathie and gave her the update.

"I love you!" she said before she hung up.

Katie's mom was calling my mother as they wheeled me out of the room, and then Katie and her mom were walking alongside the team up until they got to the doors of the operating room, where the staff stopped the stretcher so I could say goodbye.

I was feeling all kinds of emotions–happiness, excitement, fear, and nerves–all at once. I gave Katie's mom a hug, said, "I love you," and then did the same to Katie, though to her I also added, "Don't let Eric go to his father's." Then, they wheeled me to the pre-op room so they could prepare me for the surgery of my life, from whence I was given some medicine in my IV. I immediately started feeling more relaxed, and then they wheeled me to the operating room.

The next thing I knew, I was waking up with a tube in my throat.

I remember the nurse saying my mother was here in the waiting room... and then I heard the same nurse's voice saying they were going to take the tube out, which they had to do slowly because I was initially having much difficulty breathing on my own. Once this was done, the nurse gave me an ice chip, from which point I became very cold and started shivering.

It was now that I asked for my mother, so the nurse went off to find her. She returned with the news that my mother was sleeping in the waiting room and wouldn't wake up. "Can you tell me your name, where you are and why, and the day?" she pressed on.

"Karen Rosner. Duke. For a heart transplant. And it's Sunday."

"Yep, you got it!" (Well, the day was almost right: it was actually 3AM on Monday morning.)

I ended up staying in the CCU for a few days because I was having problems with my new medications; they were going right through me. The nurses would clean me up, and a couple of minutes later, they'd have to change me again. My diarrhea was so bad that the skin on my behind was getting very red, and the nurses were afraid of my skin breaking and me getting an infection as a result.

Somewhat predictably, I went into rejection within the first week of my transplant due to my diarrhea, which meant none of the medications were staying in my system long enough to actually work. I wasn't too worried about this, however: I'd read that ninety percent of heart transplant patients go into rejection within the first ninety days post-procedure. I told the doctor I was just getting it out the way early.

They had to give steroids via IV for five days as well as a course of oral steroids. These were quite unwelcome because they meant I couldn't sleep: I'd take some pain medication at 10PM, and at 10:30PM I'd take a sleeping pill, which allowed me to sleep for about three hours each night, if I was lucky.

After the team figured out what medication was causing me to have the diarrhea, they switched to another medication–and, sure enough, that symptom stopped, and the rejection was reversed.

Five days after my surgery, I was transferred to the regular floor. I also learned from the doctors around this time that before I'd awoken from the surgery, I'd actually had to go back into surgery because I'd had blood clots and was bleeding. The aim of this second surgery, if you will, was to stop the bleeding and clear the blood clots as much as possible. So, now that I was on the regular floor, Dr. Rogers came to see me every morning. (And yes, my mom was also with me every day.) This was very welcomed by me, since Dr. Rogers is a wonderful doctor, though I must admit he was also the king of bad jokes, which I'm not convinced he knew! (Well, not the "bad" part, anyway.) He always had a smile when he came in my room in the morning, and he had a great bedside manner.

On one of these days, Dr. Rogers came into my room and asked me if there was anything wrong.

"One of my staples has become loose," I admitted.

"I hope it isn't the one holding the heart in. If you wake up with your heart on your pillow, call the nurse!"

"You think?" I said and laughed.

I glanced over at my mom, who was looking *very* worried. "He was joking, Mom," I said, and she exhaled in relief and started laughing.

Another day when Dr. Rogers came in to see me, I was sitting in a chair, and he asked me to get back into bed so he could examine me. While I was laying there, he made a comment about my ankles being small.

"That's good."

"Why is it?" he asked.

"Because it means I'm not retaining fluid."

"Oh! Yes, right!" He laughed.

"Who's the doctor here, you or her?" my mom joked.

At one point, when I started really getting better, I went for a walk down the hall. Dr. Rogers was at the desk and, registering my presence, said, "They're right."

"Excuse me?"

"They're right. You can't keep a good woman down."

I smiled and said, "Thank you."

And he was right, of course.

I had another minor setback before I was discharged from the hospital: I had a fluid buildup in my lungs due to my not keeping my body moving directly after the surgery. The doctors prescribed Lasix for this, a diuretic which allowed me to get rid of the extra fluid. I also had a friend of mine come visit me during this time—the pastor I mentioned earlier. He'd had a heart transplant six months before I did, and so his presence was *extremely* reassuring and validating. I wasn't the only one going through this, and there were people out there who could fully relate to and talk me through how I was feeling.

This visit was a few days after my transplant, and he asked me to hold out my hand for him. I did, and he immediately said, "You need more Prograf [an immunosuppressant medication]. Your hand is steady."

About five minutes after the pastor left, Dr. Rogers came in and informed me they'd had to increase my Prograf intake.

"Did the pastor tell you to come in and say that?" I asked.

He frowned. "No. We did it because your levels were low."

The pastor clearly knew what he was talking about!

About one week later, the pastor returned to visit me and asked me to hold out my hand again. I obliged, and, sure enough, it was trembling. "There! You have enough Prograf now," he smiled.

That pastor helped me through several rough spots during my first-year post-transplant, and he'd also been a great help right before my transplant: I'd spoken with him for over an hour when I was initially put on the transplant list, and just speaking to him was really reassuring and validating. He was right in the fact that the worst part of getting a transplant is *waiting* to get the transplant.

There was one night after the surgery when I was in my hospital room and couldn't sleep because of the steroids. I found my mind wandering to my donor, and it was then that it fully sank in that someone had had to *die* so I could live. I wept for my donor's passing, and from that moment, I referred to my donor as

"April" in my mind, since that was the month when I'd received her heart. I told "April" that her heart was full of love from her family and friends, and that I'd fill it with even *more* love from my family and friends who cared for me. I also thanked my donor for giving me the gift of life. I told her I would treasure it, care for it, and make new memories with it.

After having that time to "speak" to my donor, I felt much better. Of course, many people who have transplants get emotional afterwards when they consider the cause for their blessing. It's a normal part of the processing period.

The day before I was discharged from the hospital, my coordinator completed an educational session with my mom, Katie, Katie's mother, and my friend, Debbie. My coordinator briefed them on my diet, incision care, activity levels, and what to look for with regards infection. She also gave an overview of my medications and my schedule, as well as of my clinic appointment schedule. Debbie asked about sexual activity, and my coordinator stated that she'd discuss that with me privately. Not that I was too concerned about that, anyway. I'd just had a heart transplant; sex was one of the last things on my mind!

When I did meet with my coordinator privately, I asked her some questions about my old heart, and I learned that its ejection fraction just before the transplant had been eight percent. In other words, I'd been rapidly getting to a point where I'd have been too sick to go through the transplant. I also signed a document giving my consent to give my heart to science so they could research it and learn how to prevent others from going through what I'd had to go through.

The only thing I regret about my transplant is the fact that I didn't ask to see my old heart. If you request to see your old heart pre-transplant, they save it for you so you can see it before they donate it, and I now regret not jumping to that opportunity for closure. All in all, though, the transplant was a success, and I felt truly blessed to have emerged basically unscathed.

The next day—May 5, 2006—I was discharged. This was my parents' anniversary, and I thought this to be a great gift.

It turned out that after I'd had my surgery, my mom had called everyone to let them know the surgery was a success... everyone except my father, who she'd somehow totally forgotten to call. Hence, upon my discharge, my sister called me to see if I could call Dad to let him know I was okay. Thankfully, Mom called Dad immediately and apologized for not calling him sooner.

Mom stayed with me for two days after I was discharged, after which my brother, Allen, took her place for a few days. Allen took me out to eat and went grocery shopping for me, and he also helped me get my blood pressure cuff working.

After Allen left, Katie and her mom took over. I also had friends from church visiting me and bringing me food, which was incredibly kind and helpful.

I couldn't drive for six weeks after my transplant, nor could I sit in the front seat just in case there was an accident, and the air bags went off (which would break my sternum again). Hence, I sat in the backseat whenever I got in the car, and sometimes, when we were running errands, my friends would take my car, so it wasn't sitting around for too long.

I was always eager to accompany my friends as they ran their errands; I was desperate to get out. One time, my friend, Maria, called me and said, "I'm going to—"

"Yes!" I interrupted.

"Let me finish."

"Okay."

She resumed: "I'm going to the grocery store and to do some other errands. Do you want to come?

"Yes."

"Okay." She laughed. "I'll be there in about thirty minutes."

It was nice to get out of the house and get some fresh air, though this also tired me out. This was only around three weeks post-surgery, after all.

The worst part of this post-transplant period was the side effects that came with all the new medication. I had a constant headache from the moment I opened my eyes in the morning all the way until I closed them at night, and I had tremors due to the Prograf. I could barely write my name; the trembling was so bad. This meant my mother had to sign several checks from my account during this time (she was on my checking account before she left my house).

One thing I did the day I came home from the hospital was turn off my cell phone and put it in my dresser drawer for two months. I didn't want to carry it around for a while. I'd had to have it with me 24/7 before the transplant, so now, I didn't want to worry about it. I still had a landline, mind, so if people wanted to get in touch with me, they could call the landline.

Of course, Eric had been staying with his father while I recovered from the transplant, and he finally came back to live with me when school was out for the summer in late June. Soon after, we went to get his driver's licenses (specifically, his restricted license. In North Carolina, when kids get their license for the first time, it has restricted times), and during the application process, the DMV officer asked Eric if he wanted to be an organ donor (it was something he had to disclose on the application form), and Eric looked up at me and smiled. I smiled back.

"What was that about?" the officer asked, curious.

"I had a heart transplant two months ago," I explained.

The officer nodded and said to Eric, "Son, you better be an organ donor, or you'll be *walking* home today!"

The three of us laughed, and Eric said, "Yes, I've been one for years."

Six months after my transplant, I started volunteering at Duke with heart transplant patients. I'd go in to speak with the patients that were being put on the list or had just had a transplant, sometimes spending an hour or more with one patient because they had so many questions. I didn't answer medical questions, of course, though I think my answers helped to reassure them, nonetheless. It was great talking with people who were going through the same thing I had. It gave them hope, like it did me when the volunteers came to my room after my transplant.

One day, I was volunteering in the cardiac waiting room, helping the visitors, when one man I was speaking to asked if I minded if he asked me some questions.

"No, not at all," I said encouragingly. "I just don't answer medical questions, but anything else is fine."

"Okay." He paused. "When did you have your transplant?"

"Six months ago."

"How long did it take you to start feeling better?"

"Well, everyone is different, and some people recover faster than others. But for me, I felt better about three months after the surgery due to the side effects of the medications."

"But when did you start feeling normal?"

"I'll get back to you on that one."

He smiled, and I chuckled.

"There's a new normal after transplant," I offered.

He thanked me for speaking with him—and that is a conversation that has stuck in my mind as pretty representative of what my role was like.

In total, I volunteered for Duke for about a year and a half before I (finally) went back to work at a medical insurance company in February 2008—a role I was offered immediately after my interview. I was thrilled about this, and immediately called Kathie to let her know I'd got the job.

I worked for that company for eight years.

All was coming together.

12
AS MY LIFE CONTINUES

In June 2008, I was able to see Eric graduate from high school. Just two years before, I hadn't thought I'd be seeing him graduate at all (read: heart condition and drug addiction), and so I felt so unbelievably lucky and proud to be there in that moment.

And yet.

Eric was using heroin and was arrested on my birthday that same year—just three months after I watched him collect his diploma, all smiles. When this happened, I did the hardest thing a mother has to do: I kept him in jail. I wouldn't bail him out this time; I'd done so once before, after he was caught shoplifting, and he'd clearly learned nothing. So, when Eric called me that day and asked me to talk to his father and ask him for help, I told him that I *would* be talking to his father, but not to ask him to help bail him out.

In truth, I felt better knowing where he was instead of him being out somewhere nondescript in the streets. This may sound strange to anyone who doesn't have any experience dealing with a drug-addicted family member, but I've learned since that this is a very common (and understandable) feeling when you've spent so long wondering where they are, what could be happening to them, and whether they're even alive or okay.

Eric was in jail for twenty-eight days, and I of course visited him during this time. It was difficult seeing him there, but I honestly think it was better for him.

I was also at his court hearing, which Eric attended with a public defender for a lawyer. He was released into my custody that day, though he was on probation, which meant he had to regularly see his probation officer, where he was regularly drug tested... but I quickly realized they were testing him for the wrong drugs. I informed the officer of this during a meeting I'd arranged so we could transfer Eric's case to Florida, since Chris and I were going to send him to rehab down there. "I bet you a week's paycheck that if you tested Eric for heroin, he wouldn't pass the test," I told them. So, she called Eric in for testing the next day, and, sure enough, he failed the test, which added another year to his probation period.

Eric was not happy, but I was doing it to save his life.

Around this time, I also found a lawyer named Michael that could help get Eric to rehab legally. When Eric and I went to see him, his advice was, "Send him to Florida. I can't help a dead client."

Chris agreed to the plan, and we paid several thousand dollars for the rehab.

While he was there, we couldn't talk to him for a little over a week, which was difficult, but the rehab seemed to be helping... until it wasn't, and then Eric was back on the drugs. Then, he got himself help, and then he fell back into the trap, and so on and so forth.

This went on for twelve years. Twelve long, troubling, heartbreaking years. I would not wish what we experienced during this time on anyone.

In among all of this stress and heartbreak, "April" (my donor) had remained on my mind ever since I had gone through my heart transplant, and so I wrote to my donor's family three times (about once a year from a little after my first-year post-transplant). Once I finished writing each letter, I'd send it to the agency that handles donations in my area (Carolina Donor Services), who would read the letter to make sure nothing too personal was in it before sending it to the family.

After the third letter I sent, I received a letter from Carolina Donor Services stating that my donor's sisters would like to talk with me. They had provided their phone numbers.

I called the first sister, incredibly nervous as I dialed. Her name was Joyce. As the phone started to ring, my nerves skyrocketed. Then, she answered with a sweet,

"Hello?"

"Hi. I'm Karen. I received your sister's heart."

There was silence on the line.

Say something! Anything! Just say something! I panicked in my head. It was probably only a second or so later when Joyce said "hi" again, but it felt like hours.

"Is this a good time?" I asked carefully.

"I just got home and was about to eat dinner. Could you call back in an hour?"

"Yes, of course."

So, I did, and the call was a little easier this time. We spoke for about an hour and a half, during which she explained a little about my donor before telling me, "Sandra's heart went to the right person."

That made me very happy to hear.

I still email Joyce occasionally.

She recommended a movie she said I should rent (*Something the Lord Made*) and when I watched it, I discovered it was about one of the first surgeries I'd had when I was a baby. I also called Joyce's other sister and found that call a little easier. We also spoke for an hour and a half, and, funnily enough, she also told me that my donor's heart went to the right person. She shared that Sandra's organs had almost not been donated, but that their mother had eventually conceded and set the ball in motion. She'd initially been against it, but the sisters had tried to talk her round, since Sandra had voiced her wanting to be an organ and tissue donor.

In the end, the mother changed her mind, Sandra became a donor, and I got a new lease on life. I'm so glad Sandra made her wishes known to her sisters. And I'm also glad that I received that letter back from them. Sometimes, when transplant recipients write to the donor's families, they don't receive a response, but, as we know, I'm someone who doesn't give up, and I *really* wanted information about my donor.

Before these phone calls to my donor's sisters, I'd had *some* information about my donor; I'd asked my coordinator they were male or female, and she'd responded, "The donor was a male, but I'm lying." (Coordinators were not supposed to provide you with any information that could enable you to identify the deceased, but I found a way.)

"How old was she?"

"Pl=]us or minus your age by ten years."

Then, I got a new coordinator, who I was able to get more information from. "So, was my donor male or female?"

"Female."

"I heard my donor was from New York but was here for vacation."

"No, she lived in the area."

"How did she die?"

"A gunshot to the head."

"I heard she was ten years plus or minus my age."

"She's ten years your senior."

With this information under my belt, I was able to go to the office of clerks downtown and find the donor's death certificate (since these are technically public records), and, sure enough, I found Sandra's death record.

When I came across it, I was stunned, and I didn't know what to do; I just stared at that page for a while. I was happy to learn a little about my donor and was even happier when her sisters were happy to divulge about her some more.

This regular contact allowed me to find some closure for my post-surgery guilt/emotion and was one of the best things I ever did.

Over Christmas in 2011, I went to Rome with Kathie, which was, of course, a great trip: I saw the Sistine Chapel and was taking pictures of the ceiling when I got lectured by a security guard; I saw Vatican City and the Colosseum, Pantheon, Trevi Fountain, and St. Peter's Basilica. I now know why they say Rome wasn't built in a day: because there are too many stairs in that city!

Unfortunately, I did become ill during that trip. I thought it was a yeast infection, but when I started taking medication from a drugstore to treat it, it didn't help, and, due to my immune system being suppressed, the infection rapidly worsened. We had passes to the midnight mass at the Vatican, but we couldn't make it due to how sick I had gotten... which should hopefully demonstrate how unwell I was really feeling!

When I got home, I went straight from the airport to the hospital because of how bad I was feeling. It turned out the yeast infection was really bad, and they had to give me IV fluids and antibiotics to manage it. I hadn't been drinking as much as

I should have been because it hurt so much that I was in tears when I urinated.

I had to take another week off work to get over this infection, and in that week, I was in the ER twice and at my doctor's office once to get this infection under control.

Not a fun thing to happen on any vacation!

This didn't stop us from continuing our travels, however. Kathie and I did a trip across the country in 2015, much like the one Chris and I had gone on all those years before. We hit a lot of the U.S.'s most well-known landmarks throughout our journey. It would have been a perfect trip had it not been for the fact that whenever Kathie and I traveled together, one of us would for some reason always either get sick or break something. And this time, it was my turn.

We were having fun and laughing, trying to navigate a raft on the river in Yosemite National Park, when we suddenly got caught under a bush and started going in circles because our rowing wasn't in sync. It's a good thing we rented the raft for three hours, since the fact we couldn't stop laughing meant it took us exactly that amount of time just to get down the river!

Well, our fun soon came to an abrupt end. While we were walking to the parking lot (where our car was), I had a mishap. Kathie was walking in front of me, and a woman passed between us both. I stepped to the side to avoid running into her, and when I did, I lost my footing and fell, hard. I looked down, to find my ankle was twice its normal size and throbbing mercilessly with pain. It was pretty obvious I couldn't put any weight on it.

Two other women, who'd been walking by and noticed me crumpled on the ground, cradling my swollen ankle, were kind enough to help me up and onto the bus, where Kathie was already seated. (I'd called for her after I'd fallen, but she hadn't heard me, continuing obliviously on.)

Once the bus journey was done, I headed straight to the clinic at the park, and I was told there that it was sprained (they didn't do X-rays). They then handed me a pair of crutches and sent me on my way.

The next day, I was in a lot of pain. Our next stop was Lake Tahoe, and I can officially confirm that Lake Tahoe has a very nice emergency room and some very good-looking doctors! More importantly, they confirmed, as I'd suspected, that my ankle was actually broken, *not* just sprained. With that, they set my ankle and put a splint on it... which meant our two-week vacation swiftly turned into a two-month vacation. I'm sure some people would've been frustrated by this, but to me, this was just another adventure, and I enjoyed my extra time off!

Kathie and I had also gone on a cruise to Hawaii the year before. Our first port call was Honolulu, and one of my core memories from that pitstop was made when we were in line for an excursion. As we stood waiting, I realized the line next to us was *really* long, and so, naturally, Kathie and I were curious over where the excursion was going. "I'll go look at the sign at the beginning of the line so I can find out," I told Kathie–and when I went to look, I couldn't believe my eyes. "You will *not* believe where that line is going," I said to her when I returned.

"Where?"

"Are you ready for this? *Walmart!*" I laughed. "I paid for a cruise to see *Hawaii*, not *Walmart!*"

Of course, the rest of that cruise proved far more interesting than I'm sure the Walmart excursion was (no offence to the people who went!). We did a port call to the Big Island (the Hilo side), Kauai, and Maui. I also did a zipline excursion in Kauai. In fact, I had seven goes on the line in total, though the first time, the guide had to give me a push because I couldn't push off hard enough to make it to the other side (I was on my tiptoes once I was hooked up!), and I screamed all the way across. Yet it was amazing–and beautiful, what with the forest below and the view of the ocean over the trees.

Clearly, I enjoyed this trip very much, because I moved to Hawaii two years later (to Honolulu), where I lived for four years. During my time there, I rappelled off a forty-story building for the Special Olympics. The event was called Over the Edge, and I had two very good incentives for doing it: two nice-looking firemen on either side of me! Plus, four other people went down the building at the same time on four different lines, which was motivating. And it was also *so* cool to see the ocean from a whole new perspective–though I did get stuck on around the seventh floor. I was hanging in the air, and the people who control the lines had to help me get... unstuck. Besides that, it was an incredible experience!

Amazingly, Eric followed suit with the move to Honolulu five months after I left, and I'm so happy to say that shortly after this move, he sought help, and has now been clean from heroin for five years.

It's amazing watching him grow.

Things haven't always been smooth sailing with Eric, of course. He's made some bad decisions in his life (as a lot of people do), and it hurt me knowing he, the little boy who I'd risked my life to have, was doing this to himself. Those twelve years spent dealing with Eric's drug issue were certainly very difficult for me, to put it lightly. As a matter of fact, this period was torturous: I didn't–*couldn't*–allow Eric to stay with me for close to two years, nor did I give him any money. If he needed food, I bought him food, but having him live with me or giving him money for him to spend however he pleased was out of the question. Basically, I did what I could for him, but I was very conscious over maintaining my decision to not enable his behavior. I did not want him in my home, but I always loved him, and when he called, I always answered.

Now, however, Eric is living in Hawaii and works as a case manager for the homeless, and so I'm *incredibly* proud of him and how he's turned his life around. I couldn't be more happy or relieved. That said, I of course still worry about him. It turns out my mom was right all those years ago: you *do* continue to worry about your kids, even when they're grown and independent.

My point in sharing these (deeply personal) details about my life is, I would like to really demonstrate the fact that even though I had severe health issues, I also had to deal with the issues that crop up all the time in the lives of people who *don't* have a severe chronic medical condition. Don't get me wrong, being born with medical issues doesn't (and shouldn't) exempt you from dealing with life's ups and downs, but when I think back to all the "normal" things I've been through in my life–my marital problems; my financial stress; raising a child who ended up hooked on drugs–and then consider the fact that I did this *while* fighting severe health issues and constantly dipping in and out of hospital (*and* having a heart transplant), it really drives home to me quite how strong and resilient us humans can really be. We are truly unstoppable in the face of conflict, if we choose to be, and I don't know about you, but that is a choice I will continue making for myself, day after day after day.

I went skydiving (again) in Hawaii for my friend's birthday some years after the first time I did it. There were five of us this time, and we went up to fifteen thousand five hundred feet. I knew before I did this that I lived on a small island, of course, but when I was freefalling, it looked *so* tiny. One good gust of wind, and I could have been shark food!

So, yes, I don't keep my feet on the ground for very long, and I've had a lot of great experiences since my transplant.

Not all that has happened since my transplant has been good, however: in January 2020, my mother passed away due to Lewy body dementia. She'd entered hospice the month before, and upon receiving news of this, I flew back home to Massachusetts to be with her. I usually don't go back to Massachusetts in the winter (I *hate* the cold and snow with a passion), but I did it for Mom. I stayed with her every day from 8AM until 8PM without fail. She didn't talk much and slept often, but I just didn't want her to be alone.

When I left her on January 3 to go back to Hawaii, I knew it would be the last time I'd see her.

Believe me when I say nothing can prepare you for a moment like that.

As I write, it's been three years since she passed, and it still hurts, but it's getting a little easier. Then again, I don't think a day will ever go by when I don't miss talking to her. I used to call her every day, whether for a five-minute or a thirty-minute conversation—whatever she was up for.

I look just like her, and so I see her every time I look in the mirror. I never used to be able (or wanted) to see the resemblance when I was younger, but now, it's all I can see, and in a way, I'm really grateful for that.

Mom had a good life, and she's missed every day.

Some months later, in July 2020, during the peak of the COVID-19 pandemic, I moved from Hawaii to Scottsdale, Arizona, since I'd lost my job in Hawaii and a mutual friend was willing to rent me her mobile home while she and her husband were away for the summer. So, I moved to Arizona, the literal *desert*, in the middle of July, when it was one hundred and seventeen degrees out. I felt like my skin was melting off me. By September, I had a job at a local hospital as a social worker (before that point, I'd kept up with a temporary job).

In January of 2022, I ended up in hospital for two days—the first time since my transplant—due to COVID-19. This was the result of my manager at the time placing me on the COVID floor of the hospital I worked at, despite the fact that she knew I couldn't be relegated to the COVID floor because I'm immunosuppressed. "That's where I need you," she told me simply, and so that's where I went. I tried to get myself off that floor, of course, but I was also wary of pushing it too much and losing my job.

I was on that floor for just four days before I started displaying the symptoms, and I ended up out of work for three weeks and in hospital for two days due to my coughing and breathing difficulties.

I did report the incident to HR, of course, but they didn't do anything about it. My doctor wrote a letter stating I wasn't ever to be on a floor with COVID-19 patients, yet the day I returned, they put me on a floor where they had seven confirmed cases of COVID-19. I reported this to HR, and the next day, I was thankfully put on a floor without COVID patients, and remained on that floor until I changed positions the following April.

I now work as a social worker for a local hospital in their liver transplant clinic, and I *love* this job: I get to help patients through the transplant journeys, which is perfect for me, since transplants are my passion, and I can build a rapport with my patients by sharing my own transplant journey with them. I think they find it reassuring to speak with someone who was once in the same position as them and so fully understands what they're going through.

Clearly, I'm very happy that Chris guided me to social work. I've now been a social worker for thirty-five years (and counting!), and every day is incredibly rewarding. A stroke of Fate, perhaps...

In a nutshell, it's been sixteen years since my heart transplant, and I'm doing well. I went skydiving again for my second transplant anniversary, I've gone on a few more cruises, and I've volunteered (and still do volunteer) for Donate Life. I feel it is really very important to be an organ, tissue, and eye donor: one person can save up to eight people's lives with organ donations and improve up to sixty people's lives with tissue donation. A no-brainer!

Recently, I had to have a stent put in my heart due to a blockage—not due to my eating habits and not because of my heart, which is unusual. Thus, I'm currently going through cardiac rehab again, for the fourth time in my life. I don't mind doing this, however. Something I do find amusing is that the first time I was in cardiac rehab, I was in my twenties, while the other participants were in their fifties and up; the second time, I was in my thirties, so the gap seemed to close a bit; the third time (after my transplant), I was in my forties, and, again, the gap was closing; and now, I'm fifty-nine, so I've (finally!) caught up with the other participants.

I know that as I continue, I will only grow stronger (and possibly make new friends), and I meanwhile run my own side business: I empower women who are forty and older to gain control of their finances and get out of debt. I love seeing my clients feeling financially empowered and living a life of less financial stress. I've gone through the stress of debt after my divorce, after all, as well as when I lived in Hawaii, when I lost my job. I was able to get out debt after my divorce, however, and I'm working through my debt from Hawaii. I've paid off eighty percent of it, and as I write, will be debt free by March 2023 (or sooner), which is a huge achievement!

My point is, I learned a lot from that experience, and I want to share my experience and help others to get their debt under control. Getting into debt is far easier than getting out of debt, after all: you need to work hard, stay on track, learn new behaviors, and have an accountability partner that will tell you "No" even when you want to hear "yes"—and that is what I do for my clients. I'm with my clients throughout their entire journey to being debt free, whether in person or via Zoom.

I also have a non-profit foundation, which has been an incredible experience. My entire adult life, I've been serving and helping people (as you can easily see from my career so far), yet I haven't quite been satisfied with this alone. I want to help people even when I'm no longer here. Thus, I set up my non-profit so I could help transplant patients, and, to bring that vision to life, sixty percent of the profits from this book will go to my non-profit (the Your New Lease on Life Foundation) for this cause!

Transplants are expensive before, during, and after the procedure: before, the transplant patient undergoes a lot of testing and attends several medical appointments just to get clear (and we ladies also have to go through a couple more tests than our male counterparts); during the transplant are the copayments of being in hospital; and then after the transplant, the copayments for medication can total up to thousands of dollars per month. And, of course, there are co-pays for medical appointments and tests. Because of this, I see patients struggling to pay for medication daily, and it is these patients that my non-profit endeavors to help. I was fortunately able to get help with my medication payments after my transplant, and among those was one medication that I had to take for four months, the co-pay for a thirty-day supply of which being one thousand four hundred dollars. That was almost as much as my rent at the time—and when people are on a limited income, it's even harder for them to make ends meet.

My goal in launching my foundation is to help as many patients as possible every year—and then keep increasing its impact! My foundation helps anyone in the U.S. who is in the process of being evaluated for a transplant, all the way to two years post-transplant.

The foundation Your New Lease on Life not only assists patients with co-pays for medications, but it also helps them find resources so the patient can receive all the support they need now *and* in the future. We also provide resources that help with medication manufacturing companies who assist with medication co-pays, assistance with Medicare and Medicaid applications, and support groups.

I see this foundation helping transplant patients all over the country. I would also like to hire patient volunteers at the foundation. In the meantime, one thing is for sure: when they approach our foundation, the patient will *not* be bounced around from one person to the next. If the patient starts working with me, that patient will be working with me for the next two years, end of.

And the best part is, for a patient to start getting assistance with our foundation, all they have to do is make one simple phone call!

This leads us to our big question: why did I write this book?

Well, I wrote this book so I could provide some solidarity and inspiration to anyone going through a similar health journey to that which I've been through. After all, you can get through anything in life with the right mindset and determination. My motto is, "They said I couldn't. That's why I did," and every birthday I've celebrated has proved those first doctors' prognoses wrong by one more year!

I know not many people hold this sentiment about getting older, but I love watching the years go by. It's better than the alternative!

Here's to many more years of memory-making and pushing on, despite the odds.

Oh, and if you were wondering: I still have Mrs. Beasley. She doesn't have her glasses, apron, or bib anymore, but she's still in one piece, which counts for something (I did first get her in 1966, after all). She also doesn't talk anymore–one of my brothers cut the string a long time ago–but when I look at her, I remember my childhood spent in hospital so vividly.

I obviously moved several times after that first move to college, and so Mrs. Beasley wound up in another box for years. A few years ago, when I was making yet another move, I was going through some old stuff when I found Mrs. Beasley stuffed in a box. Unable to resist that face and the memories that went with it, I took her out, and since then, she's been back on my bed during the day... and on the floor at night.

I've considered having her restored several times, but I must admit I'm afraid to have her with someone else, just in case they lose her. Like I said, she's been with me throughout my childhood, and I was never very keen on having anyone else whisk her away!

I recently looked up how much Mrs. Beasley would be worth today. On eBay, she's going for between ninety and one hundred and fifty dollars. I believe my mom paid about ten dollars for her back in 1966. So, I'll keep her around for a little while longer.

Just for that reason, of course.

ACKNOWLEDGMENTS

I would like to thank my family and friends who have helped me through the hard times in my life. I couldn't have gotten through those things without your help.

I also want to thank all the doctors and nurses that have cared for me throughout the years.

And a special thanks to my donor, Sandra, and her family, for giving me the gift of life. If Sandra hadn't donated her heart, this book wouldn't be in your hands right now.

If you would like to assist with the Your New Lease on Life Foundation, you can do so at https://ynlolfoundation.org–and if you have any questions about KMR Personal Financial Coaching Services, head on over to www.facebook.com/groups/kmrpersonalfinancialservices.

Thank you again for reading. It has been a joy sharing my story with you!

ABOUT THE AUTHOR

Karen M. Rosner has a master's degree in social work and is currently a transplant social worker for a local hospital. She also runs a personal financial coaching business and a non-profit for transplant patients.

Karen was raised with six brothers and a sister in Massachusetts, and when she became an adult, she chased the warm weather and found it in Arizona. Before settling in Arizona, however, Karen lived in Pennsylvania, Virginia, North Carolina, and Hawaii.

Karen has a son–her miracle child that came into her life after she was told she would not be able to have children.

Karen's mantra is the quote by Jimmy Butler, "They told me I couldn't. That's why I did." Karen believes her purpose is to serve and love the people that come into her life and is therefore committed to helping those in need.

www.ynlolfoundation.org

www.facebook.com/groups/kmrpersonalfinancialservices

kmrpfc22@gmail.com

808-253-1157

www.ingramcontent.com/pod-product-compliance
Lightning Source LLC
La Vergne TN
LVHW050958080826
845145LV00009B/2350

* 9 7 8 1 9 1 3 2 0 6 5 4 3 *